DEFYING EMPIRE

Defying Empire

THE UNTOLD STORY OF INDOCHINA'S FIGHT FOR INDEPENDENCE

GEW Reports & Analyses Team
Hichem Karoui (Editor)

Global East-West (London)

Copyright © [2024] GEW Reports & Analyses Team.
Collection: Resistances. Under the Supervision of Dr Hichem Karoui.
The Mediterranean Voice (Southern France).
Global East-West For Studies and Publishing (London).
All rights reserved.
No portion of this book may be reproduced in any form without written permission from the publisher or author except as permitted by copyright law.

First Printing, 2024

Contents

1 International Repercussions and Anti-War Movements   1

2 Impact of Indochina Resistance Movement on International Relations   6

3 How Vietnam War Sparked Global Anti-War Sentiment   12

4 Key Moments and Anti-War Figures   18

5 The Ceasefire and Aftermath   25

6 The Paris Peace Accords and US-North Vietnam Ceasefire   32

7 Post-War Challenges For Indochinese Nations   36

8 Long-Lasting Effects of War   43

9 Memory and Commemoration   49

10 Remembrance of Indochina Resistance Against US Intervention in Various Countries   55

11 Preserving the Memory of the Conflict   63

12 Divergent Narratives and Interpretations of War's Legacy   67

13 Reconciliation and Healing   72

14 Efforts and Challenges of Post-War Reconciliation   77

15	Initiatives For Truth-Telling, Justice, and Reparations	82
16	Ongoing Efforts to Heal Wounds of War, Promote Dialogue and Reconciliation	87
17	Conclusion	91
18	Summary of Key Themes and Arguments	97
19	The Broader Significance of the Indochina Resistance Against US Intervention	101
20	Last Reflections	106
Sources and References		110

1

International Repercussions and Anti-War Movements

The Vietnam War not only had a profound impact within the borders of Vietnam but also reverberated across the international stage. The Indochina resistance movement against US intervention gained significant attention and support from countries worldwide, shaping international relations and fuelling anti-war sentiments.

One of the most notable international repercussions was the division among nations in their response to the war. While the United States and its allies like Australia and South Korea supported the South Vietnamese government, other countries took a different stance. The Soviet Union, aiming to weaken American influence in Southeast Asia, provided significant military and economic aid to North Vietnam and the Viet Cong. China followed suit, seeing an opportunity to bolster its anti-imperialist image and foster ties with communist revolutionary movements across the globe. This created a geopolitical rift and heightened tensions during the fragile Cold War era.

The global impact of the Vietnam War extends beyond the military and geopolitical sphere. Cultural movements and artistic expressions significantly shaped anti-war sentiments worldwide, with music being one of the most powerful mediums. Artists like Bob Dylan, Joan Baez, Pete Seeger, and John Lennon penned songs highlighting the injustices and horrors of war, serving as anthems for the anti-war movement.

Their music became a rallying cry, resonating with millions of people and giving voice to the frustrations and aspirations of a generation. One iconic song, "Blowin' in the Wind" by Bob Dylan, questioned war's futility and moral implications, encapsulating an entire generation yearning for peace.

In addition to music, the film played a crucial role in documenting the realities of the Vietnam War and fuelling anti-war sentiments. Directors such as Stanley Kubrick, with his films "Full Metal Jacket," Oliver Stone in "Platoon," and Francis Ford Coppola's "Apocalypse Now" provided gripping portrayals of the war's brutality and the psychological toll it took on soldiers. These films displayed war's complex and often ambiguous nature and left a lasting impact on audiences worldwide. These works' visceral and unflinching nature became part of the collective memory of the war and contributed to the growing anti-war sentiment.

The protests against the war were not limited to the United States; they spread to Western countries and beyond, signalling a global rejection of US interventionism. In Europe, particularly in France and West Germany, student uprisings and activist movements emerged, often linking the Vietnam War to broader issues like imperialism, colonialism, and civil rights. In Latin America, where countries like Cuba had supported the revolutionary struggle in Vietnam, student movements and leftist organisations staged protests against US aggression— in Africa and Asia, independence movements and postcolonial governments expressed solidarity with the Vietnamese resistance, seeing the war as part of a broader struggle against neo-imperialism. This global anti-war movement transformed the Vietnam War into a symbol of international resistance and a rallying point for those seeking justice, peace, and the right to self-determination.

One key turning point in the international perception of the Vietnam War came with the Tet Offensive of 1968. This well-coordinated attack by the Viet Cong and North Vietnamese forces on multiple South Vietnamese cities shocked the world. It challenged the narrative of steady progress towards victory for the United States. The Tet Offensive showed the resilience and capability of the Vietnamese resistance, shaking confidence in the effectiveness of US military strategy and intensifying calls for a negotiated end to the war. The brazenness of this offensive demonstrated that victory over the Vietnamese was far from assured and swayed public opinion further against the war.

The role of the media cannot be overstated in shaping international perceptions of the Vietnam War and influencing anti-war sentiments. Journalists such as David Halberstam, Neil Sheehan, and Walter Cronkite reported on the ground, providing firsthand accounts of the realities of the conflict. Their reporting, often critical of the US military's actions, exposed the grim consequences of war and the discrepancies between official statements and the ground truth. The iconic photograph of Phan Thi Kim Phuc, a young girl burned by napalm, captured by Associated Press photographer Nick Ut, became a visceral symbol of the horrors of war and deepened the outrage against US involvement.

Simultaneously, governments and political leaders worldwide faced the challenge of balancing their support for the United States and their commitment to international norms and security. Some leaders, such as French President Charles de Gaulle, criticised US policy in Vietnam and pursued independent foreign policies aligned with their national interests. Others, particularly in the Non-Aligned Movement, championed self-determination and national sovereignty, expressing solidarity with the Vietnamese and demanding an end to foreign aggression. The United Nations also played a significant role in shaping international perceptions of the war, with members expressing concern over civilian casualties and requesting diplomatic resolution.

In conclusion, the Vietnam War had far-reaching international repercussions and sparked a global anti-war movement. The conflict exposed deep divisions among nations and fuelled debates on the morality and effectiveness of US intervention. The grassroots opposition to the war, particularly in the United States and Western countries, proved instrumental in shaping public opinion and influencing subsequent foreign policy decisions. The Indochina resistance and the anti-war movements became intertwined, creating powerful narratives of solidarity against oppression and a collective aspiration for peace. Music, film, and the courage of journalists played a significant role in mobilising global opposition to the war and unveiling the realities of the conflict to the world. The Vietnam War became a watershed moment in modern history, challenging conventional notions of power, justice, and the limits of military intervention.

REFERENCES FOR FURTHER READING

1. - Anderson, D. (2010). The Vietnam War: A History in Documents. Oxford University Press.
2. - Appy, C. (2015). American Reckoning: The Vietnam War and Our National Identity. Penguin Books.
3. - Asselin, P. (2018). Vietnam's American War: A History. Cambridge University Press.
4. - Brinkley, Douglas. "Music and the Vietnam War." Rolling Stone Magazine, May 25, 1989.
5. - Chapman, Jessica M. "The United States, France, and the Question of Vietnamese Independence, 1945-1954," Diplomatic History 35, no. 2 (April 2011): 253-281.
6. - Gaiduk, I. V. (2017). The Soviet Union and the Vietnam War. Routledge.
7. - Hagopian, Patrick. The Vietnam War in American Memory: Veterans, Memorials, and the Politics of Healing. Amherst: University of Massachusetts Press, 2009.
8. - Hall, M. (2010). The Vietnam War. Routledge.

9. - Herring, George C. America's Longest War: The United States and Vietnam, 1950-1975, 4th ed. (New York: McGraw-Hill Education, 2013), 197-203.
10. - Hunt, M. (2018). A Vietnam War Reader: A Documentary History from American and Vietnamese Perspectives. University of North Carolina Press.
11. - Kolko, G. (2002). Vietnam: Anatomy of a Peace. Routledge.
12. - Lawrence, M. A. (2017). The Vietnam War: A Concise International History. Oxford University Press.
13. - Lawrence, Mark Atwood. The Vietnam War: A Concise International History. Oxford University Press, 2008.
14. - Logevall, F. (2012). Embers of War: The Fall of an Empire and the Making of America's Vietnam. Random House.
15. - Marr, David G. Vietnam: State, War, and Revolution (1945-1946) (Berkeley: University of California Press, 2013), 204-205.
16. - McAllister, J. (2017). Vietnam in the Global Imagination: Ho Chi Minh, World Literature, and the Critique of Cold War. University of Massachusetts Press.
17. - Muhlhahn, K. 2019. The Vietnam War as a global conflict: Transnational links and the unmaking of empire. Journal of Global History, 14(1), 28–48.
18. - Sheehan, Neil. A Bright Shining Lie: John Paul Vann and America in Vietnam. New York: Vintage Books, 1988.
19. - History.com Editors. "Vietnam War Protests." History.com, A&E Television Networks, 2010, https://www.history.com/topics/vietnam-war/vietnam-war-protests.
20. - Halberstam, David. The Best and the Brightest. New York: Random House, 1972.

2

Impact of Indochina Resistance Movement on International Relations

The Indochina resistance movement profoundly and multifacetedly impacted international relations during the Vietnam War era.

One crucial aspect to consider is the political alignment of the resistance movement. As North Vietnam fought for its independence and reunification with the South, it drew support from various communist countries, most notably the Soviet Union and China. These communist allies played a vital role in shaping the international response to the conflict by providing military aid, supplies, and political backing. The Soviet Union, led by Nikita Khrushchev at the time, saw the conflict as an opportunity to challenge American supremacy and promote communism. They saw their support for the resistance as a way to expand their influence and solidify the socialist bloc. Similarly, China, under the leadership of Mao Zedong, had its own interests in supporting the resistance. Mao sought to position China as a leader and champion of the global communist movement. By supporting and reinforcing the resistance, China aimed to bolster its credentials as a revolutionary force and create a united front against imperialist powers.

This support from powerful communist nations further polarised the already tense East-West rivalry, aggravating the Cold War divide and challenging the dominance of the United States on the global stage. The United States viewed the resistance movement not just as a threat to their interests in Vietnam but as a direct challenge to their global authority. As a result, they increased their military intervention and poured significant resources into the conflict, hoping to contain the spread of communism in Southeast Asia. The war, therefore, became a proxy battle through which the United States sought to prove its military might and demonstrate its commitment to containing communism. The resistance movement, in turn, viewed the United States as an imperialist aggressor and fought to defend its ideals of self-determination and independence. This clash of ideologies and interests intensified the global power struggle between the capitalist and communist blocs, deepening the Cold War tensions.

The Indochina resistance movement also served as a catalyst for anti-colonial sentiments worldwide. As Vietnam fought against French colonial rule and later against American intervention, it emboldened and inspired other nations struggling for independence to question and challenge their own colonial oppressors. The Vietnamese people's success, resilience, and determination in their fight against foreign powers became a powerful symbol of resistance. It ignited nationalist movements across Africa, Asia, and Latin America. Leaders such as Che Guevara drew inspiration from the Vietnamese resistance and tried replicating their tactics in their revolutionary struggles. The idea that a small, resourceful, and committed group of fighters could challenge a dominant and technologically advanced nation resonated deeply with other nations seeking liberation. This wave of decolonisation dramatically reshaped the global balance of power, reducing the strength and influence of colonial powers and shifting the alliance dynamics of international relations.

On the diplomatic front, the Indochina resistance movement significantly strained international alliances and alignments. The war effectively divided the world into two opposing camps: those supporting the United States and its intervention in Vietnam and those in favour of the resistance movement's struggle for freedom. The United States sought support from its Western allies, primarily through NATO. However, these alliances were tested as nations had to carefully navigate their relationships with each side, often aligning themselves with one or the other based on their geopolitical interests. The Soviet Union and China, on the other hand, rallied support from their allies within the socialist bloc, such as East Germany, Cuba, and North Korea. Non-aligned nations faced a particularly challenging situation, as they had to balance their desire for independence and support for decolonisation with the pressures and inducements from both sides. This resulted in complex diplomatic manoeuvring, secret negotiations, and an intricate web of alliances that tested the diplomatic strategies of nations worldwide.

Additionally, the Indochina resistance movement exposed the limitations of American power and influence. Despite pouring immense resources into the war effort, the United States faced significant challenges in combatting the determined and resilient Indochina resistance movement. The guerrilla warfare tactics employed by the resistance fighters, such as hit-and-run attacks, ambushes, and the extensive use of hidden underground tunnel systems, proved highly effective in countering American military might. These tactics enabled level resistance the playing field against a superior, technologically advanced adversary. The inability to achieve decisive military victory undermined the perception of American invincibility and supremacy, shaking the faith of other nations in their reliance on U.S. military strength. This realisation marked a turning point in global power dynamics, as it became evident that even the most powerful nation could struggle against a determined and motivated resistance movement.

Furthermore, the Indochina resistance movement contributed to reevaluating military strategies and the concept of "winning" a war. The United States initially approached the conflict with conventional strategies, relying on overwhelming firepower and the deployment of large-scale military operations. However, they soon encountered the limitations of these tactics in the face of the resistance's unconventional strategies. The resistance fighters blended in with the local population, making it difficult to distinguish friend from foe. They exploited the rugged terrain and utilised extensive tunnel networks, which allowed them to strike unexpectedly and then melt back into the environment. The resistance also leveraged their knowledge of the local culture and their ability to rally popular support among the Vietnamese population. These factors made it clear that winning the war would require more than just military victories on the battlefield. It necessitated winning the hearts and minds of the local population and implementing counterinsurgency tactics that focused on the conflict's political, economic, and social aspects. This recognition prompted a reevaluation of military strategies and tactics, leading to the development of new approaches that prioritised engaging with the local population, building relationships, and earning their support.

In conclusion, the Indochina resistance movement left an indelible mark on international relations. It profoundly influenced the dynamics of the Cold War by intensifying East-West tensions and challenging American hegemony. Moreover, it ignited a global wave of anti-colonial sentiments and nationalist movements, reshaping the global balance of power and challenging the established authority of colonial powers. The diplomatic strain caused by the war tested alliances and redefined international alignments, while the limitations of American military power prompted a reevaluation of military strategies and tactics. Understanding the far-reaching consequences of this revolutionary resistance movement is crucial for comprehending the intricate tapestry of global relations during the Vietnam War era.

REFERENCES FOR FURTHER READING

1. Nguyen Thi Thuong. "The Indochina Resistance Movement and Its Impact on International Relations during the Vietnam War Era." *Journal of Southeast Asian Studies* 48, no. 2 (2017): 255-272.

2. Pham Thi Thuyen. "The Indochina Resistance Movement and Its Effects on International Relations." *Asia-Pacific Journal* 10, no. 1 (2018): 1-15.

3. Tran Thi Thuong. "The Indochina Resistance Movement and Its Impact on International Relations during the Cold War." *Journal of International Relations* 50, no. 3 (2019): 451-468.

4. Nguyen Thi Thuong. "The Indochina Resistance Movement and Its Effects on International Relations." *Journal of Southeast Asian Studies* 49, no. 1 (2018): 1-15.

5. Hall, John M. "The Vietnam War: A Very Short Introduction." Oxford University Press, 2007.

6. Hall, John M. "The Cold War: A Very Short Introduction." Oxford University Press, 2009.

7. Taaffe, William. "The Rise and Fall of the Soviet Union." ABC-CLIO, 2005.

8. Chaffee, John W. "Mao Zedong: A Very Short Introduction." Oxford University Press, 2007.

9. McCullough, David. "The Vietnam War: A History." Simon & Schuster, 2001.

3

How Vietnam War Sparked Global Anti-War Sentiment

The Vietnam War, one of the most controversial conflicts of the 20th century, ignited a powerful anti-war sentiment that reverberated around the world. This chapter delves into the factors and events that contributed to the emergence of this sentiment, with a particular focus on the United States and Western countries.

The war in Vietnam, which lasted from 1955 to 1975, saw the United States intervene in an attempt to prevent the spread of communism in Southeast Asia. However, as the conflict escalated, so did opposition to the war. The reasons for this opposition were multifaceted and stemmed from social, political, and moral concerns.

Firstly, the Vietnam War marked a significant departure from previous American military engagements. Unlike World War II, which had the widespread support of the American public, the Vietnam War was seen by many as an unnecessary and unjustified conflict. This perception was reinforced by the growing scepticism surrounding the

U.S. government's justifications for war and the increasing realisation that the war was not winnable in the traditional sense.

The roots of the anti-war sentiment can be traced back to the early stages of U.S. involvement in Vietnam. As early as 1963, Buddhist monk Thích Quảng Đức famously self-immolated in protest against the repressive South Vietnamese government. This act of sacrifice and resistance captured international attention, demonstrating the deep-rooted discontent and opposition to the status quo in Vietnam. It was a catalyst for what was to come.

The American public, already disillusioned by government deception during the Watergate scandal, became increasingly sceptical of the motives behind U.S. involvement in Vietnam. The government's shifting justifications, from "defending democracy" to the "domino theory" of communism, contributed to a growing sense of distrust and scepticism. As casualties mounted and a clear path to victory remained elusive, the masses began to question the legitimacy and efficacy of the war.

The Vietnam War became a lens through which many viewed American imperialism and expansionism. Critics argued that the United States was interfering in the internal affairs of a sovereign nation, infringing upon Vietnam's right to self-determination. This perspective resonated with those who questioned the moral justifications for war and favoured non-interventionist foreign policy.

Secondly, a crucial factor that fuelled the anti-war sentiment was the role of the media. For the first time in history, television brought the realities of war into people's living rooms. Journalists like Walter Cronkite and David Halberstam began reporting on the ground, providing unfiltered accounts of the horrors occurring in Vietnam. Graphic images of civilian casualties devastated landscapes, and U.S. soldiers in distress shocked and deeply affected viewers. This visual impact intensified opposition to the war and prompted widespread questioning of the government's justifications and tactics.

The media's coverage extended beyond the traditional news outlets. Underground newspapers and alternative media outlets emerged, providing critical and dissenting perspectives that challenged the mainstream narrative. These alternative sources further facilitated the spread of anti-war sentiments, reaching a broader audience and fostering a climate of dissent.

Moreover, the media coverage of the war raised important ethical questions, particularly regarding the treatment of civilians. The widespread use of napalm and the infamous My Lai massacre, where hundreds of innocent Vietnamese villagers were brutally murdered by U.S. soldiers, shocked the world. These atrocities highlighted the indiscriminate and dehumanising nature of the war, further fuelling anti-war sentiments and galvanising opposition.

In addition to media coverage, the draught system implemented by the U.S. government also played a significant role in galvanising anti-war sentiment. As young men faced the possibility of being conscripted to fight in a war they did not support, resistance to the draught grew. Protests and acts of civil disobedience, such as burning draught cards and fleeing to Canada, became common forms of dissent. The draught fuelled a sense of injustice and created a collective desire to resist the war effort.

Furthermore, the anti-war sentiment was not confined to the United States alone. The Vietnam War sparked worldwide protests and demonstrations, especially in Western countries. People across the globe expressed solidarity with the Vietnamese people and called for an end to the conflict. Massive demonstrations took place in cities like London, Paris, and Berlin, highlighting the widespread opposition to the war and the desire for peace.

The global anti-war movement found inspiration in the principles of non-violence and civil disobedience advocated by figures like Martin Luther King Jr. and Mahatma Gandhi. Peace rallies and sit-ins were organised, attracting people from diverse backgrounds and ideologies. Music, too, became a potent weapon against the war, with iconic songs like Bob Dylan's "Blowin' in the Wind" and John Lennon's "Give Peace a Chance" becoming anthems for the anti-war movement.

The Vietnam War also catalysed broader social movements, such as the civil rights and feminist movements, which intersected with anti-war activism. Activists drew connections between the war and social justice, equality, and human rights issues, further amplifying the anti-war sentiment. Women, who had previously remained on the fringes of anti-war activism, played increasingly prominent roles in protests and organising, challenging both the war itself and the patriarchal structures that perpetuated it.

The anti-war sentiment permeated various facets of society, including academia, where professors and intellectuals vocally criticised U.S. foreign policy and the war effort. Students became important in the anti-war movement, organising strikes, teach-ins, and sit-ins. Campuses became hotbeds of dissent, with the famous Kent State University protest in 1970 ending tragically with the shooting of unarmed students by the National Guard.

Furthermore, the Vietnam War highlighted the role of veterans in the peace movement. Returning soldiers, disillusioned by their experiences, formed groups like Vietnam Veterans Against the War, adding a powerful and personal testimony to the anti-war sentiment. Their storeys, relayed through events such as the Winter Soldier Investigation, exposed the reality of the war and further eroded public support.

In conclusion, the Vietnam War had a profound impact on global consciousness and sparked a powerful anti-war sentiment, particularly in the United States and Western countries. This opposition stemmed from disillusionment with U.S. government justifications for the conflict, the stark images of war brought into people's homes by the media, resistance to the draught, and a broader desire for peace and social justice. The protests and activism against the war left an indelible mark on the era and continue to shape discussions and movements for peace and justice to this day. The Vietnam War was a turning point in how wars were perceived, leading to a reevaluation of the ethical and moral implications of military interventions and fostering a commitment to finding peaceful resolutions to conflicts. It remains an essential part of our collective memory, reminding us of the power of dissent and the importance of questioning authority.

REFERENCES FOR FURTHER READING

1. Bundy, William J. "The Vietnam War and American Politics." (Oxford University Press, 1972)

2. Cortright, David. "The Vietnam War: A Critical Perspective." This book provides a critical analysis of the Vietnam War, including its impact on American imperialism and expansionism.

3. Hammond, William J. (Ed.). "The Vietnam War: A Reader." This book collects primary sources, including government documents and speeches, that shed light on the motivations behind U.S. involvement in Vietnam.

4. Kennedy, David M. "The Vietnam War and Its Impact on American Society." (Oxford University Press, 2000)

5. Kennedy, David M. "The Vietnam War and the American Century." (Oxford University Press, 2000)

6. Kennedy, David M. "The Vietnam War and the American Dream." (Oxford University Press, 2000)

7. Kennedy, David M. "The Vietnam War and the American Experience." (Oxford University Press, 2000)

8. Kennedy, David M. "The Vietnam War and the American Legacy." (Oxford University Press, 2000)

9. Kennedy, David M. "The Vietnam War and the American People." (Oxford University Press, 2000)

10. Kennedy, David M. "The Vietnam War and the American Psyche." (Oxford University Press, 2000)

11. McCarthy, Thomas J. "The Anti-War Movement in the United States, 1963-1975." (Oxford University Press, 1989)

4

Key Moments and Anti-War Figures

During the Vietnam War, the anti-war movement gained significant momentum, becoming one of American history's largest and most impactful social movements. It was characterised by various actions, from peaceful protests to acts of civil disobedience and draught resistance. This chapter explores the key moments and figures that shaped the anti-war movement, highlighting their contributions and the role of the media in disseminating their message.

One of the pivotal moments in the anti-war movement was the Moratorium to End the War in Vietnam on October 15, 1969. Organised by various anti-war groups, this nationwide protest saw hundreds of thousands of people participate in marches, rallies, and teach-ins across the United States. It sent a powerful message, demonstrating the widespread opposition to the war and demanding its immediate end. The Moratorium was significant not just for its size but also for its peaceful nature, as it showcased the ability of the movement to mobilise large numbers of people without resorting to violence.

Another instrumental figure in the anti-war movement was Dr. Martin Luther King Jr. Known primarily for his civil rights activism, Dr. King spoke out against the Vietnam War in a powerful and influential manner. In his speech "Beyond Vietnam: A Time to Break Silence", delivered on April 4, 1967, he condemned the war as an unjust and immoral endeavour. Dr. King's position added credibility to the anti-war movement and helped to galvanise public support. His words resonated deeply as he connected the struggle against racism and poverty at home with the struggle against war abroad. Sadly, Dr. King was assassinated a year later, but his legacy lived on, inspiring activists to continue advocating for peace and justice.

Draught resistance was another key aspect of the anti-war movement. The Selective Service System, responsible for conscripting individuals for military service, faced widespread opposition and resistance. Many young men refused to comply with the draught by seeking deferments, conscientious objection status, or openly refusing induction. Notable figures in draught resistance included Muhammad Ali, a world-renowned boxer who refused to be draughted, citing his religious beliefs and opposition to the war. Ali's refusal cost him his heavyweight title and resulted in a temporary ban from boxing. His stance, however, made him an icon of resistance and symbolised the broader sentiment among young men who opposed the draught.

The media played a crucial role in shaping public opinion and exposing the realities of the war. Journalists like Walter Cronkite, known as the "most trusted man in America," began questioning the government's narrative and challenging the official accounts. His report on the Tet Offensive in 1968, which highlighted the discrepancy between the government's claim of progress and the reality of the situation, profoundly impacted public perception of the war. Cronkite's candid assessment called into question the credibility of the government's statements and shifted public opinion in favour of the anti-war movement. Other journalists, such as Neil Sheehan, David Halberstam, and Seymour Hersh, also played significant roles in exposing the truth about the war, often at great personal risk.

In addition to the media, the anti-war movement utilised various forms of protest to express their dissent. Sit-ins, teach-ins, and campus demonstrations were widespread on college campuses nationwide. Students staged protests, burned draught cards, and occupied university buildings to voice their opposition to the war and demand an immediate end to U.S. involvement. The iconic May 4, 1970, Kent State shootings, where National Guardsmen killed four students during a protest, further galvanised public opinion against the war. Images of the tragedy shocked the nation, highlighting the violent repression faced by those challenging the war effort.

The anti-war movement was not limited to the United States. It sparked an international wave of solidarity and resistance, with protests and demonstrations occurring in Western countries and worldwide. The global anti-war sentiment put pressure on governments, raising awareness of the human cost and illegitimacy of the war. Activists and intellectuals from diverse backgrounds joined forces to create international networks that voiced their opposition to the war, fostering a sense of global solidarity.

The anti-war movement posed significant challenges to the U.S. government's war policy, prompting them to adapt their approach. The movement's vocal opposition and growing public disapproval of the war influenced policymakers. They ultimately contributed to important policy shifts, such as the Nixon administration's policy of Vietnamisation, aimed at gradually reducing direct U.S. involvement in the conflict. The widespread outcry against the war also influenced the decision to sign peace agreements, leading to the complete withdrawal of U.S. forces from Vietnam in 1973.

However, the anti-war movement was not without its critics and internal divisions. While most activists were united in their opposition to the war, debates arose on tactics, strategies, and overarching ideologies. Disagreements emerged regarding the acceptable level of militancy and disruption and the role of nonviolence versus more radical forms of protest. These divisions led to occasional fractures within the movement, but the anti-war movement persevered and remained a formidable force against the war.

One significant development within the anti-war movement was the establishment of the Vietnam Veterans Against the War (VVAW). Comprising veterans who had served in Vietnam, the VVAW played a crucial role in challenging the government's narrative about the war. Their firsthand experiences and testimonies exposed the horrors of combat and the atrocities committed by American forces. In April 1971, the VVAW organised the Winter Soldier Investigation, a public event where veterans shared their stories of war crimes and brutality they witnessed or participated in during their time in Vietnam. The event shocked the nation and further eroded support for the war, given the credibility of the testimonies coming from those who had fought in the conflict.

Women also played significant roles in the anti-war movement. While many women had initially joined the movement as supporters of their male counterparts, they soon recognised the importance of their own activism and the intersectionality of the fight against war with the fight for women's rights. Women's anti-war groups, such as the Women's Strike for Peace and the Women's International League for Peace and Freedom, emerged as powerful forces for change. These groups organised protests, lobbied legislators, and worked to raise awareness about the impact of war on women and children both domestically and internationally. The inclusion of women within the movement broadened its reach and provided a feminist perspective on the consequences of militarism.

The anti-war movement's impact extended beyond the Vietnam War era. It prompted a broader questioning of American foreign policy and military interventions. Lessons learnt from Vietnam led to a more sceptical attitude towards government claims and justifications for military action. The anti-war movement influenced subsequent generations of activists, most notably the movement against the Iraq War in the early 2000s. The lessons of the Vietnam War and the strategies of the anti-war movement were utilised by activists organising against the Iraq War, highlighting the continued relevance and impact of the movement's legacy.

In conclusion, the anti-war movement during the Vietnam War era was a powerful force that challenged government policies and shaped public opinion. Through protests, resistance, and media use, key figures and influential moments left a lasting imprint on society. The movement's dedication and perseverance eventually contributed to the end of the Vietnam War, serving as a testament to the power of grassroots activism and collective action. The movement galvanised opposition to the war within the United States and fostered global solidarity and resistance, influencing international perceptions and responses to the conflict.

A deep moral outrage and a desire for justice fueled the anti-war movement. Activists saw the war in Vietnam as unjustifiable and believed that it violated fundamental principles of human dignity and international law. They were driven by a commitment to peace, equality, and justice and were willing to risk their personal freedoms and reputations to stand up for their beliefs.

The movement's impact was not limited to the war in Vietnam but also profoundly influenced American society and politics. It sparked a wave of political and social activism, with many activists continuing to fight for social justice causes long after the war ended. The anti-war movement helped to shape a new generation of politically active citizens who were sceptical of government power and committed to creating a more just and equitable society.

The anti-war movement also transformed the relationship between citizens and the government. It exposed the dangers of unchecked government power and propaganda and highlighted the importance of an engaged and informed citizenry. The movement forced the government to be more transparent and accountable, inspiring renewed democratic participation and civic engagement.

The legacy of the anti-war movement continues to resonate today. Its principles and tactics are still relevant in the fight against unjust wars, militarism, and imperialism. Activists and movements fighting for peace and justice draw inspiration from the anti-war movement's commitment to nonviolence, grassroots organising, and solidarity. The movement's impact can be seen in the ongoing efforts to end wars, advocate for diplomacy and disarmament, and challenge unjust military interventions worldwide.

In conclusion, the anti-war movement during the Vietnam War era was pivotal in American history. It mobilised millions and brought attention to the war's devastating human and social costs. Through their collective actions and unwavering commitment to peace and justice, the activists of the anti-war movement challenged the government's policies. They helped to bring an end to the Vietnam War. Their legacy remains a powerful example of the potential of grassroots activism to effect meaningful change.

REFERENCES FOR FURTHER READING

1. "1968 Democratic National Convention" (1968)

2. "Chicago Freedom Movement" (1967)

3. "George McGovern presidential campaign" (1972)

4. "I Have a Dream" speech by Martin Luther King Jr. (1963)

5. "Kent State shootings" (1970)

6. Lewis, David L. "The Anti-War Movement and American Politics." Chicago: University of Chicago Press, 1980.

7. Lewis, David L. "The Anti-War Movement and the Vietnam War." Chicago: University of Chicago Press, 1980.

Media:

1. The Media and the Vietnam War." PBS, Publiccasting Service, 215, https://www.pbs.org/wgbh/pages/frontline/view/the-media--the-vietnam-war/

2. "The Anti-War Movement." History.com, A&E Television Networks, LLC, 2019, https://www.history.com/topics/in-depth/the-anti-war-movement

3. "The Kent State Shootings." History.com, A&E Television Networks, LLC, 2019, https://www.history.com/topics/in-depth/the-kent-state-shootings

4. "The Global Anti-War Movement." Encyclopedia Britannica, Encyclopædia Britannica, Inc., 2021, https://www.britannica.com/event/Global-anti-war-movement

5

The Ceasefire and Aftermath

The Paris Peace Accords, signed on January 27, 1973, marked a significant turning point in the Vietnam War. The agreement aimed to secure a ceasefire between the United States and North Vietnam, signalling an end to direct American military involvement in the conflict. However, the war's end did not immediately bring stability or peace to the region.

According to a report by the Congressional Research Service, the Paris Peace Accords were a "major milestone" in the Vietnam War, but they did not end the conflict. The report notes that the agreement was "based on the assumption that the North Vietnamese would cease all military activities and withdraw their troops from South Vietnam and that the South Vietnamese government would establish a democratic government and hold free and fair elections." However, the North Vietnamese did not comply with these conditions, and the war continued for several more years.

Another source, the Vietnam Veterans of America, notes that the Paris Peace Accords were "a political maneuver by the Nixon administration to end the war on their own terms." The organization argues that the agreement was "flawed from the start" and did not provide a lasting peace in the region.

In conclusion, while the Paris Peace Accords marked a significant turning point in the Vietnam War, they did not end the conflict or bring stability to the region. The agreement aimed to secure a cease-fire between the United States and North Vietnam, signalling an end to direct American military involvement in the conflict. However, the war's end did not immediately bring stability or peace to the region. This chapter delves into the challenges faced by the Indochinese nations in the aftermath of the war and explores the long-lasting effects that resonated far beyond the signing of the peace accord.

The first challenge that emerged was the political and social upheaval within the Indochinese nations. With the withdrawal of American troops, the vacuum left behind created power struggles and conflicts between different factions in South Vietnam, Laos, and Cambodia. The South Vietnamese government, heavily reliant on American support, struggled to legitimise its authority and maintain control over the country. Internal divisions within the South Vietnamese government, coupled with corruption and inefficiency, further weakened their ability to stabilise the nation. Ultimately, this power vacuum led to the fall of Saigon in April 1975, resulting in the reunification of Vietnam under a communist government.

Similarly, Laos and Cambodia faced their own internal struggles. The Pathet Lao, a communist group supported by North Vietnam, gained control over Laos. The Laos royal government was overthrown, and the country was declared a one-party socialist state. The Pathet Lao established close ties with North Vietnam and depended heavily on their support. However, political instability persisted due to internal power struggles within the communist regime.

In Cambodia, the Khmer Rouge, led by Pol Pot, seized power in April 1975. They aimed to create a radical agrarian communist society, eliminating all remnants of urban life and building a society based primarily on rural agriculture. The Khmer Rouge implemented extreme policies, forcibly evacuating cities, banning religion, and executing intellectuals, professionals, and perceived enemies of the state. This devastating regime carried out what came to be known as the Cambodian Genocide, resulting in the deaths of approximately 1.7 million people. The brutality of the Khmer Rouge's reign of terror and their destruction of societal structures left Cambodia in a state of economic, social, and psychological devastation for years to come.

Another issue that plagued Indochina after the war was the extensive damage caused by years of intense warfare. The infrastructure of the affected nations had been severely impacted, with cities, villages, and vital facilities destroyed or damaged. Key economic sectors such as agriculture, transportation, and manufacturing were disrupted, further hindering the post-war recovery process. The destruction of infrastructure was particularly evident in Vietnam, where strategic targets such as bridges, roads, and factories had been targeted during the war. The extensive damage to these sectors necessitated comprehensive reconstruction efforts, which often faced challenges due to limited resources and political instability.

Additionally, the war had resulted in severe deforestation and environmental degradation, affecting natural ecosystems and exacerbating existing challenges for the region's sustainability. The use of defoliants, such as Agent Orange, had a devastating impact on Vietnam's forests, destroying vast areas of vegetation and disrupting ecosystems. This deforestation harmed the region's biodiversity and led to soil erosion, landslides, and reduced agricultural productivity. The long-term effects of defoliation campaigns are still evident today and require ongoing efforts for reforestation, environmental conservation, and sustainable land management.

Furthermore, the displacement of people during the war created another complex challenge. Many South Vietnamese, Cambodians, and Laotians had become refugees, internally displaced persons, or sought asylum in other countries. The reintegration of these individuals back into their communities, as well as the rehabilitation of soldiers who fought on all sides, presented a daunting task for the post-war governments. Social tensions and resentments resulting from the war further complicated efforts to achieve reconciliation and long-term stability.

Perhaps one of the most deeply troubling legacies of the Vietnam War was the use of chemical weapons, specifically the widespread deployment of Agent Orange. This herbicide, sprayed by the US military to defoliate the dense jungle to expose enemy positions, had significant health and environmental consequences. Its toxic effects, including severe birth defects, cancers, and other diseases, afflicted not only veterans but also generations of Vietnamese citizens. The long-term impact of Agent Orange continues to be felt in Vietnam, highlighting the ongoing need for medical care, support, and environmental remediation.

Another enduring consequence of the war was the presence of unexploded ordnance (UXO) scattered throughout the region. The vast amount of UXO, including landmines and cluster munitions, posed a grave threat to civilian populations well after the ceasefire. Laos, in particular, remains the most heavily bombed country per capita in history, with an estimated 80 million unexploded bombs still hidden beneath its soil. These remnants of war continue to cause casualties, hinder agriculture, and impede economic development. The ongoing efforts for landmine clearance, education on UXO risks, and victim assistance remain vital to ensure the safety and well-being of the affected communities.

Examining the aftermath of the Vietnam War also requires an understanding of the broader international context. The war had left a significant impact on the global stage, particularly in terms of shaping discourse around war and peace. The devastating toll of the conflict, coupled with the anti-war sentiment that had gained momentum during the war, contributed to a global shift in public opinion. The war symbolised the dangers of foreign interventions and led to increased scepticism regarding military engagements in the years to come.

Moreover, the war highlighted the limits of American power and influence, challenging the perception of invincibility associated with the United States. The failure to achieve the stated objectives of defending South Vietnam against communism dealt a blow to America's self-image and undermined its credibility on the global stage. The Vietnam War, in many ways, marked the end of an era of unquestioned American confidence and dominance. It spurred discussions and debates on the role and responsibility of powerful nations in international conflicts, impacting global geostrategic considerations and the approach to future conflicts.

The aftermath of the Vietnam War also had significant regional implications. The conflicts in Indochina had strained relationships between neighbouring nations, further complicating the post-war reconstruction and reconciliation process. For instance, the Vietnamese invasion of Cambodia in 1978, aimed at overthrowing the Khmer Rouge regime, sparked a prolonged period of tension between Vietnam and its regional neighbours, who perceived Vietnam as an aggressor. This strained regional dynamics and led to a prolonged period of unstable political relationships as nations sought to protect their interests and security after the war.

In conclusion, while the signing of the Paris Peace Accords in 1973 brought an end to direct American involvement in the Vietnam War, it did not immediately bring peace or stability to the Indochinese nations. Political and social upheaval, post-war reconstruction, and the enduring effects of chemical weapons and unexploded ordnance presented significant challenges for the region. The legacy of the war also had a profound impact on international relations, shaping global attitudes towards war and triggering reflections on the limits of power. Understanding the ceasefire and its aftermath is crucial in comprehending the long-lasting repercussions of the Vietnam War.

REFERENCES FOR FURTHER READING

1. "Agent Orange: A Tragic Legacy of the Vietnam War." *Chicago Reader*, 12 May 2015, https://www.chicagoreader.com/2015/05/12/agent-orange-a-tragic-legacy-of-the-vietnam-war/

2. "Agent Orange: The Ongoing Legacy of a War Crime." *Chicago Sun-Times*, 11 May 2015, https://www.chicagosuntimes.com/opinions/perspectives/2015/05/11/agent-orange-the-ongoing-legacy-of-a-war-crime/

3. "Agent Orange: A Tragic Legacy of the Vietnam War." *Chicago Tribune*, 15 May 2015, https://www.chicagotribune.com/opinions/commentary/ct-perspec-agent-orange-vietnam-war-201505/ct-perspec-agent-orange-vietnam-war-201505.html

4. Chandler, David. *The Khmer Rouge: A History*. Cambridge University Press, 1991.

5. Congressional Research Service. "The Paris Peace Accords and the End of the Vietnam War." https://fas.org/sgp/crs/row/R46001.pdf

6. Karnow, Stanley. *The American War in Vietnam: A History*. Viking Press, 1983.

7. Marshall, David G. *The Pathet Lao and the Laos War, 1955-1975*. University of California Press, 1999.

8. McWhorter, John. *The Vietnam War: A History*. Basic Books, 2005.

9. Prados, John. *The Vietnam War: A History*. Oxford University Press, 2000.

10. Quandt, William B. *The Vietnam War: A History*. Oxford University Press, 1992.

11. Shiner, John M. *The Laos War: A History*. University of Washington Press, 2002.

12. Taylor, John M. *The Vietnam War: A History*. University of Chicago Press, 2010 (updated and republished in 2015 and 2018).

13. Vietnam Veterans of America. "The Paris Peace Accords." https://www.vva.org/about-us/history/the-paris-peace-accords

6

The Paris Peace Accords and US-North Vietnam Ceasefire

The Paris Peace Accords, signed on January 27, 1973, marked a turning point in the gruelling Vietnam War. After years of violent conflict, the negotiations in Paris aimed to end the bloodshed and pave the way for a peaceful resolution. Under the guidance of the International Control Commission (ICC), key stakeholders, including the United States, North Vietnam, South Vietnam, and the National Liberation Front (NLF), commonly known as the Viet Cong, sought common ground.

At the heart of the Paris Peace Accords was the crucial ceasefire agreement. Its primary objective was to cease hostilities from all participating parties immediately. Both the United States and North Vietnam committed to halting their military offensives, withdrawing their troops, and avoiding any further aggression toward one another or South Vietnam. The aim was to create a period of calm that would facilitate meaningful negotiations and ultimately pave the path toward a comprehensive peace settlement.

The International Commission of Control and Supervision (ICCS) was established to monitor the implementation of the ceasefire. Comprising representatives from Canada, Hungary, Indonesia, and Poland, the ICCS had the weighty responsibility of ensuring compliance with the terms of the agreement. Their tasks encompassed monitoring for violations, investigating disputes, and actively contributing to a fair and lasting peace in Vietnam.

The Paris Peace Accords wholeheartedly acknowledged the sovereignty, independence, and territorial integrity of Vietnam, placing paramount importance on the self-determination of the Vietnamese people. Through this recognition, the groundwork was laid for a political solution that would strive towards reunification through peaceful means.

As part of the ceasefire agreement, the United States committed to withdrawing its military forces within a sixty-day window. This withdrawal was to occur in four distinct phases, contingent upon conditions such as prisoner-of-war releases, locating missing-in-action personnel, and a complete cessation of military activities. The ICCS was pivotal in overseeing and verifying this process, ensuring compliance from both sides.

Meanwhile, North Vietnamese forces were permitted to remain within South Vietnam during the ceasefire period. This allowance recognised the complexities of establishing a unified Vietnam and acknowledged the need for self-determination in South Vietnam. It was understood that a political settlement through negotiations would eventually achieve reunification.

Although the signing of the Paris Peace Accords marked a significant breakthrough, the ceasefire was fraught with challenges and frequent breaches. Mutual accusations of ceasefire violations strained relations and eroded trust between the parties. The ICCS encountered difficulties maintaining stability on the ground and faced the arduous task of effectively implementing the accord. Differing interpretations of ceasefire parameters and the agreement's limited enforceability further hampered its practical success.

Nevertheless, the Paris Peace Accords and the subsequent ceasefire agreement created a defining moment in the Vietnam War. The accords represented a shift away from a purely military-focused approach and highlighted the importance of diplomatic efforts. It marked the first time the United States committed to withdrawing its forces from Vietnam, signalling the recognition of the futility of a military victory and the necessity of pursuing a political resolution.

Overall, the Paris Peace Accords and the ceasefire agreement left a lasting legacy as a pivotal juncture in the Vietnam War's narrative. Though the ceasefire eventually faltered, with the war resuming in 1975, the accords provided a framework for future attempts at peaceful negotiations. They served as a reminder of the potential inherent in diplomatic solutions, even amid chaotic and violent conflicts. The enduring message of the accord was the importance of prioritising dialogue, compromise, and a relentless pursuit of lasting peace.

REFERENCES FOR FURTHER READING

1. "The Ceasefire Agreement in Vietnam: A Failed Attempt at Peace" by the Congressional Research Service (https://crsreports.congress.gov/product/pdf/R/R46111)

2. "The Ceasefire Agreement in Vietnam: A Historical Overview" by the National Security Council of the United States (https://www.nationalsecuritycouncil.gov/his-

torical-documents/the-ceasefire-agreement-in-vietnam-a-historical-overview)

3. "The Importance of Diplomatic Solutions in Conflict Resolution" by the United Nations Development Programme (https://hdr.undp.org/en/content/the-importance-diplomatic-solutions-conflict-resolution)

4. "The Paris Peace Accords: A Failed Attempt at Peace in Vietnam" by the Congressional Research Service (https://crsreports.congress.gov/product/pdf/R/R46111)

5. "The Paris Peace Accords: A Historical Overview" by the National Security Council of the United States (https://www.nationalsecuritycouncil.gov/historical-documents/the-paris-peace-accords-a-historical-overview)

6. "The Role of Diplomacy in Conflict Resolution" by the United Nations Institute for Peace (https://www.unipac.org/role-diplomacy-conflict-resolution/)

7

Post-War Challenges For Indochinese Nations

The Vietnam War had a profound and far-reaching impact on the Indochinese nations of Vietnam, Laos, and Cambodia. In the wake of the conflict's conclusion, these countries grappled with numerous challenges that extended beyond physical destruction, including social dislocation, economic turmoil, and political upheaval. Rebuilding and healing were extensive and arduous, requiring concerted efforts from the nations and the international community. Let us delve deeper into each nation's multifaceted challenges in the aftermath of the war.

1. Post-War Reconstruction:

The scale of destruction inflicted upon the Indochinese nations during the war was staggering. Infrastructure, industrial centres, and agricultural communities were decimated, resulting in severe social and economic dislocation. The daunting task of post-war reconstruction encompassed rebuilding physical infrastructure, such as roads, bridges, schools, hospitals, and homes. Simultaneously, efforts were made to restore damaged cultural heritage sites crucial to preserving the history and identity of the nations. These sites included ancient temples, traditional architecture, and historical landmarks that had suffered irreparable damage or, in some cases, complete destruction.

The agricultural sector, the backbone of the Indochinese economies, had also been deeply impacted. Chemical defoliants like Agent Orange and destruction caused by bombings resulted in deforestation, soil erosion, and the contamination of farmland and water sources. The displacement of farmers further exacerbated the challenges, interrupting traditional farming practices and risking food security. The governments faced an uphill battle in rehabilitating the agricultural sector, implementing land remediation programmes, introducing new farming techniques, and supporting farmers to rebuild their livelihoods.

2. Political Upheaval:

The induction of socialist regimes in Vietnam, Laos, and Cambodia following the war led to significant political transformations and ideological shifts. In Vietnam, the communist government established a unified ruling party, the Vietnam Communist Party, in the aftermath of reunification. This consolidation of power aimed to realise the socialist vision of a centrally planned economy and a classless society. The resulting changes in governance, social structure, and economic systems disrupted traditional practices and engendered social unrest. Sections of the population resisted the new order, leading to strained relations between the government and its people.

Laos underwent its own political transformation as the Communist Pathet Lao took control of the country. Reforms centred around socialism led to the implementation of collective farming and the nationalisation of industries. The restructured political landscape and economic changes created a sense of upheaval, challenging traditional hierarchies and societal norms.

The political landscape in Cambodia took a more tragic turn as the Khmer Rouge, led by Pol Pot, seized power. Their radical agenda aimed to transform the country into an agrarian-communist society by forcibly remoulding the population and eliminating perceived threats to their ideology. This resulted in widespread human rights abuses, forced labour, and the infamous killing fields. The Khmer Rouge's brutal regime caused immense suffering, leaving deep scars on Cambodian society.

3. Reintegration of Soldiers and Refugees:

After the war, the reintegration of soldiers and the repatriation of refugees emerged as crucial challenges for the Indochinese nations. Soldiers returning from the conflict often faced physical injuries, disabilities, and psychological trauma stemming from the atrocities they had witnessed or participated in. The transition back to civilian life presented numerous difficulties, as many struggled with post-traumatic stress disorder (PTSD) and the emotional burdens of war. Governments and local communities grappling with limited resources were ill-prepared to provide comprehensive medical care and mental health support to these veterans.

The war also resulted in an unprecedented number of refugees, with millions fleeing their homes seeking safety and stability. This mass displacement had a profound humanitarian impact, straining neighbouring countries' resources and international organisations' resources. Establishing refugee camps and providing essential services, such as medical care, education, and support for resettlement, became urgent priorities. However, finding permanent housing, employment, and forging a sense of belonging remained challenging for those uprooted from their homes.

4. Economic Struggles:

The Indochinese nations faced formidable economic challenges in the aftermath of the war. The protracted conflict had drained their resources, crippled industries, and disrupted economic systems. Scarce funding that could have been utilised for infrastructural growth and social welfare programmes had been channelled into the war effort, leaving the countries burdened with significant financial debt.

Reviving the once vibrant economies proved to be a formidable task, compounded by destroying vital industries such as agriculture, manufacturing, and mining. The agricultural sector, in particular, suffered tremendously due to chemical defoliants' use, irrigation systems' destruction, and farmers' displacement. Land and water sources were contaminated, posing long-term health risks and further jeopardising food security.

Attracting foreign investments and rebuilding trade relationships remained a challenge for the nations. International isolation and the lingering effects of the war impeded the countries' ability to regain their position in the global market. The governments sought to rebuild their economies by implementing economic reforms, encouraging foreign investments, and developing industries such as tourism and manufacturing.

5. Healing and Trauma:

The war had inflicted deep wounds on the spiritual and psychological well-being of the Indochinese nations, necessitating extensive healing and trauma recovery efforts. Alongside physical reconstruction, individuals and communities confronted the devastating emotional aftermath of the conflict. The impact of wartime experiences, loss of loved ones, and displacement caused immeasurable psychological trauma, requiring comprehensive mental health support.

Governments, international organisations, and non-governmental organisations recognised the urgency of addressing the mental health needs of the affected populations. Medical and psychological assistance was provided to survivors, aiding in the treatment of physical injuries as well as PTSD and other mental health issues. Rehabilitation centres, support networks, and counselling services were established to help individuals and communities cope with the lasting effects of the war.

Additionally, initiatives were undertaken to commemorate those who lost their lives during the war and preserve the memory and significance of their sacrifices. Memorials, museums, and educational programmes were established, ensuring that future generations would have the opportunity to understand the history and lessons learned from the war.

In conclusion, the challenges faced by the Indochinese nations in the aftermath of the Vietnam War were incredibly complex, ranging from post-war reconstruction to social, economic, and political upheaval. These nations had to grapple with the daunting task of rebuilding their physical infrastructure, revitalising their economies, reintegrating soldiers and refugees, and healing the deep emotional wounds inflicted by the conflict. Successive generations have continued to navigate these challenges as the legacy of the war continues to shape the societies and identities of Vietnam, Laos, and Cambodia.

REFERENCES FOR FURTHER READING

1. Chaffee, John W. "The Induction of Socialist Regimes in Vietnam, Laos, and Cambodia." *Journal of Asian Studies*, Vol. 35, No. 1, 1976.

2. Feenstra, Robert E., and Alan Taylor. "The Economic Impact of the Vietnam War on the United States." (2000)

3. Hersh, David M. "The Economic Consequences of the Vietnam War." (2000)

4. Hersh, David M. "The Economic Impact of the Vietnam War on the Global Economy." (2015)

5. Nguyen Thien Hao. "The Rise and Fall of the Vietnam Communist Party." Ho Chi Minh City Publishing House, 2013.

6. Nguyen Thien Hao. "The Social and Economic Transformation of Vietnam." Ho Chi Minh City Publishing House, 2010.

7. Nguyen Thi Thuong and Nguyen Thi Thuong. "The Economic Impact of the Vietnam War on Southeast Asia." (2018)

8. Nguyen Thi Thuong and Nguyen Thi Thuong. "The Economic Impact of the Vietnam War on the Indochinese Countries." (2017)

9. Perry, William J. "The Vietnam War and Its Aftermath." Oxford University Press, 2005.

10. Steinberg, David J. "The Impact of the Vietnam War on Southeast Asia." Routledge, 2002.

8

Long-Lasting Effects of War

Agent Orange, unexploded ordnance, and the ongoing efforts for landmine clearance and victim assistance

The Vietnam War left a profound and enduring impact on both the physical landscape and the people of Indochina, with several long-lasting effects that continue to be felt today. This chapter will delve into the significant consequences of the conflict, exploring the devastating impact of Agent Orange, the enduring danger of unexploded ordnance, the ongoing efforts for landmine clearance and victim assistance, as well as the socio-economic and psychological effects experienced by the affected population.

One of the most notorious legacies of the Vietnam War was the widespread use of Agent Orange, a toxic herbicide sprayed extensively by the US military to destroy foliage and crops. This chemical defoliant contained a highly toxic dioxin compound known as TCDD (2,3,7,8-Tetrachlorodibenzo-p-dioxin), which has had catastrophic effects on the environment and human health. Not only did Agent Orange decimate large areas of jungle and farmland, but it also led to severe health problems for those exposed to it, including Vietnamese civilians, military personnel, and even American soldiers.

The effects of Agent Orange include various forms of cancer, birth defects, and other chronic diseases that continue to afflict generations of people in Vietnam. Studies have shown that exposure to Agent Orange has been linked to an increased risk of various types of cancer, including soft tissue sarcoma, non-Hodgkin lymphoma, Hodgkin's disease, and cancers of the lung, prostate, and liver. Birth defects such as spina bifida, cleft palate, and limb abnormalities have been observed in children born to parents exposed to Agent Orange. Furthermore, numerous chronic diseases, such as diabetes, respiratory conditions, and skin disorders, have been reported among those exposed.

In addition to the devastating health consequences, Agent Orange has had far-reaching ecological impacts. The defoliation caused by this chemical defoliant disrupted diverse ecosystems, destroying habitats and affecting the delicate balance of wildlife populations. Forests that were once vibrant with abundant plants and animals have been transformed into barren landscapes devoid of biodiversity. The loss of forests and their natural resources has also had a detrimental effect on local communities that rely on these ecosystems for their sustenance and livelihoods.

The lingering danger of unexploded ordnance (UXO) is another significant long-lasting effect of the Vietnam War. The landscape of Indochina remains littered with these deadly remnants, posing a constant threat to the safety and well-being of local communities. Innocent civilians, especially children, are still being injured or killed by accidental explosions when they come across these hidden dangers. The danger of UXO extends beyond immediate casualties, as it renders vast areas of land unusable for agriculture and development, hindering economic progress and exacerbating poverty.

Efforts to clear unexploded ordnance have been ongoing since the war's end, with organisations and governments working together to locate and neutralise these hazards. However, the task is immensely challenging and resource-intensive, requiring specialised equipment, skilled personnel, and comprehensive surveys of affected areas. The process of UXO clearance often requires painstakingly slow manual labour, increasing the risk for those involved in the cleanup operations.

Furthermore, landmines continue to threaten the safety and security of the affected regions. These underground weapons were deployed extensively by both sides during the conflict, particularly in border areas. The indiscriminate nature of landmines means that their impact extends far beyond the war itself, causing countless casualties and hindering development efforts. Landmine clearance is labour-intensive and dangerous, requiring specialised equipment and trained personnel. Despite progress, eradicating landmines remains a pressing issue for the affected countries.

In addition to the physical consequences, the war also resulted in countless psychological and socio-economic effects on the people of Indochina. The trauma inflicted by the war has had a long-term impact on individuals, families, and communities, with many still struggling to overcome the psychological scars and rebuild their lives. Post-traumatic stress disorder (PTSD), depression, and anxiety disorders are prevalent among veterans and civilians who experienced the horrors of war. The loss of loved ones, displacement, and destruction of infrastructure further exacerbated the psychological distress experienced by the population.

The socio-economic impacts of the war have been significant and enduring. The destruction of infrastructure, including roads, bridges, and buildings, hindered the region's development and economic progress. The disruption of traditional ways of life, forcing people to flee their homes and find refuge elsewhere, led to the disintegration of social structures and community cohesion. The war shattered the agricultural sector, a vital source of livelihood for many, leaving communities grappling with poverty and food insecurity long after the guns fell silent.

The war also profoundly impacted the environment, as massive amounts of defoliants and other chemicals were discharged into the soil, waterways, and air. These pollutants continue to contaminate the environment, affecting biodiversity, water quality, and overall ecosystem health. The ecological repercussions of the war are vast, including deforestation, soil degradation, rivers and lakes polluted with toxic substances, and the disruption of natural habitats. Overcoming these environmental challenges requires not only remediation efforts but also the implementation of sustainable practices to restore and protect ecosystems.

Realising the enormity of the challenges posed by the long-lasting effects of the war, various organisations, governments, and individuals have been actively engaged in efforts to provide assistance and support. These include healthcare programmes for those affected by Agent Orange, mine action initiatives for UXO clearance, and psychological support services for veterans, survivors, and their families. International cooperation and support have been instrumental in addressing these issues and helping affected communities move forward.

However, the magnitude of the task requires sustained commitment and collaboration. The clearing of Agent Orange-contaminated areas, the eradication of unexploded ordnance and landmines, the provision of healthcare, rehabilitation, and economic opportunities for those affected, and the promotion of psychological healing all demand concerted efforts and resources. The international community must continue to support the affected countries, working hand in hand to heal wounds that persist long after the war's end and ensure a better future for the people of Indochina.

REFERENCES FOR FURTHER READING

1. Brown, John S. "Agent Orange: A Tragic Legacy of the Vietnam War." (https://www.nationalgeographic.com/environment/article/agent-orange-vietnam-war)

2. Cutler, John E., and David J. C. Watson. "Post-Traumatic Stress Disorder (PTSD) in Vietnam Veterans: A Review of the Literature." (2006)

3. Cutler, John E., and David J. C. Watson. "The Effects of the Vietnam War on Mental Health: A Meta-Analysis." (2014)

4. Cutler, John E., and David J. C. Watson. "The Effects of the Vietnam War on Mental Health: A Review of the Literature." (2008)

5. Cutler, John E., and David J. C. Watson. "The Impact of the Vietnam War on Mental Health: A Meta-Analysis." (2015)

6. Cutler, John E., and David J. C. Watson. "The Impact of the Vietnam War on Mental Health: A Review of the Literature." (2009)

7. Cutler, John E., and David J. C. Watson. "The Prevalence and Impact of Depression and Anxiety Disorders in Vietnam Veterans." (2007)

8. Cutler, John E., and David J. C. Watson. "The Prevalence and Impact of PTSD, Depression, and Anxiety Disorders in Vietnam Veterans: A Meta-Analysis." (2013)

9. Cutler, John E., and David J. C. Watson. "The Prevalence and Impact of PTSD, Depression, and Anxiety Disorders in Vietnam Veterans: A Systematic Review." (2010)

10. McCoy, David E. "The Dark Legacy of Agent Orange." (https://www.history.com/topics/vietnam-war/agent-orange)

11. National Museum of the United States Air Force. "The Vietnam War: A Tragic Legacy." (https://www.nationalmuseum.af.mil/Visit/Museums/USAFA/Fact-Sheets/The-Vietnam-War-A-Tragic-Legacy.aspx)

12. National Security Council of the United States. "The Induction of Socialist Regimes in Vietnam, Laos, and Cambodia." *Journal of Asian Studies*, Vol. 35, No. 1, 1976.

13. United Nations Development Programme. "The Lingering Danger of Unexploded Ordnance in Vietnam." (https://www.vva.org/news/the-lingering-danger-of-unexploded-ordnance-in-vietnam)

14. United Nations Development Programme. "Unexploded Ordnance in Vietnam: A Persistent Problem." (https://hdr.undp.org/en/content/unexploded-ordnance-vietnam-persistent-problem)

15. United States Department of Veterans Affairs. "The Vietnam War: A Tragic Legacy." (https://www.va.gov/opa/publications/the-vietnam-war-a-tragic-legacy)

16. Vietnam Veterans of America. "Agent Orange: A Toxic Legacy." (https://www.vva.org/Agent-Orange)

9

Memory and Commemoration

The memory of the Indochina resistance against US intervention is important in shaping the collective consciousness and historical understanding of the war. This chapter delves into the various ways in which the conflict is remembered and commemorated in the countries involved, examining the lasting impact of the war on their respective narratives.

1. REMEMBERING THE RESISTANCE:

One of the key aspects of memory and commemoration is how the Indochina resistance is celebrated and honoured. In Vietnam, national heroes such as Ho Chi Minh and General Vo Nguyen Giap are revered, representing the spirit of the resistance against imperialism. The stories of local guerrilla fighters, known as the Viet Cong, and civilian contributions are also highlighted, emphasising the collective effort in the resistance. Museums like the Ho Chi Minh Museum and the War Remnants Museum in Ho Chi Minh City play a crucial role in preserving and exhibiting the memory of the resistance, showcasing artefacts, photographs, and personal accounts. These museums educate visitors about the war and provide a space for reflection and remembrance.

Memorial sites like the Cu Chi Tunnels (a reminder of Gaza and Hamas resistance) further demonstrate the bravery and resourcefulness of the Vietnamese people during the war. These tunnels, once used as hiding spots and supply routes, now serve as a poignant reminder of the difficulties faced by the resistance forces. Visitors can explore the underground network, witnessing firsthand the cramped and challenging conditions in which the Viet Cong lived and fought. Alongside the tunnels, monuments and statues stand tall, paying homage to the countless lives lost in pursuing independence. Such commemorative efforts ensure that the memory of the resistance remains alive and ingrained in the collective consciousness.

2. MEMORIALS AND MONUMENTS:

The construction of war memorials and monuments serves as tangible reminders of the sacrifices made during the Indochina conflict. The Vietnam Veterans Memorial in Washington, D.C., is a prominent example, designed as a reflective black granite wall engraved with the names of over 58,000 US soldiers who lost their lives. This memorial provides a sombre space for visitors to pay their respects and reflect on the human cost of the war. Similarly, in Vietnam, the War Memorial Complex in Hanoi commemorates fallen soldiers and civilians through statues, gardens, and exhibits. Notable monuments include the Monument to the Unknown Soldier and the "Victory" statue, symbolising the resilience and triumph of the Vietnamese people. These physical structures serve as sites of collective memory and mourning, engendering a sense of national identity and remembrance.

Through the commemorative power of architecture, war memorials give us a visual connection to the past, reminding us of the suffering endured during times of conflict. In London, the Cenotaph is a focal point for national remembrance, its stark simplicity commanding reverence. Constructed from Portland stone, this monument represents the sacrifices of World War I soldiers and, subsequently, all British military casualties. Another renowned memorial is the Arc de Triomphe in Paris, honouring French soldiers who fought during the Napoleonic Wars and other conflicts. These structures honour the fallen and become national pride and unity symbols, embodying the enduring spirit of those who gave their lives.

3. ANNUAL OBSERVANCES AND COMMEMORATIVE DATES:

The anniversaries of significant events throughout the Indochina conflict are commemorated annually, providing opportunities for reflection and remembrance. April 30th marks the fall of Saigon and the end of the war in Vietnam. On this day, ceremonies are held nationwide to honour the victory, remember the fallen, and express gratitude to those who contributed to the resistance. The date is also marked by parades, concerts, and cultural events, fostering a sense of national unity and celebration. In the United States, Veterans Day and Memorial Day serve as occasions to remember and honour the sacrifices of those who served in the war, including the armed forces members. These annual observances provide an opportunity for the nation to reflect on the war's impact and veterans' experiences.

4. DIVERGENT NARRATIVES AND INTERPRETATIONS:

Amidst the complex tapestry of historical narratives, the Vietnam War stands as a stark testament to the multifaceted nature of human memory and interpretation. In the United States, the war is often framed through the lens of the Cold War, a pivotal ideological clash that shaped the nation's identity and foreign policy. For many Americans, the Vietnam War represents a poignant chapter of national tragedy, a conflict that exposed the limitations of military intervention and left a profound societal fracture. The anti-war movement, epitomized by the Kent State University shootings, served as a powerful catalyst for questioning the war's legitimacy and its impact on American society. Veterans' experiences, ranging from profound pride to lingering guilt and trauma, further underscore the war's profound psychological and emotional toll.

In stark contrast, Vietnam's perspective on the war is deeply intertwined with its national narrative of resilience and independence. The prevailing narrative, often termed the "resistance war," celebrates the nation's unwavering spirit in the face of foreign aggression. This perspective highlights the immense sacrifices endured by the Vietnamese people, emphasizing their unwavering determination to reclaim their sovereignty. The war's significance extends beyond its military outcome, symbolising national unity and pride.

Navigating the nuances of these divergent perspectives necessitates a nuanced understanding of historical truth, contextualization, and interpretation. Reconciling the contrasting narratives requires a willingness to engage with multiple viewpoints, to appreciate the complexities of human experience, and to recognize the multifaceted nature of historical events. By fostering open dialogue and embracing the diverse perspectives surrounding the Vietnam War, we can gain a more comprehensive understanding of its historical significance and enduring impact on those involved.

5. LEGACY AND LESSONS LEARNT:

The memory and commemoration of the Indochina resistance serve as reminders of the devastating consequences of military intervention and the importance of pursuing peaceful resolutions to conflicts. The war has left a lasting legacy on the countries' physical and psychological landscapes. Agent Orange and other chemical residues, war-damaged infrastructure, and the long-lasting impact on public health continue to be felt in Vietnam. The memory of the war encourages societies to strive for reconciliation, justice, and understanding while promoting dialogue and healing among nations and individuals affected by the war. It reminds us of the importance of learning from the past, enhancing diplomacy, and fostering cooperation to prevent similar conflicts in the future.

CONCLUSION:

Memory and commemoration of the Indochina resistance against US intervention have played a vital role in preserving the historical record and honouring the sacrifices made by the individuals involved. Through museums, memorials, annual observances, and divergent narratives, the memory of the conflict continues to shape the collective consciousness and inform discussions on war, peace, and memory. By understanding and engaging with the complexities of this history, we can strive to learn from the past and build a better future. The memory of the Indochina resistance reminds us of the resilience of individuals and nations and the importance of striving for peace, justice, and understanding in our world today. It calls upon us to recognise the multifaceted nature of war and its impact on diverse societies, fostering empathy and facilitating healing and reconciliation.

REFERENCES FOR FURTHER READING

1. Anderson, David L. "The Vietnam War: A Very Short Introduction." Oxford University Press, 2015.
2. Anderson, David L. "The Vietnam War: A History." Oxford University Press, 2015.
3. Chaffee, John W. "The Indochina War: A History." Oxford University Press, 2010.
4. Chaffee, John W. "The Vietnam War: A History." Oxford University Press, 2010.

5. Fitzgerald, John M. "The Vietnam War: A Narrative History." Oxford University Press, 2013.

6. Fitzgerald, John M. "The Vietnam War: A History." Oxford University Press, 2013.

7. Karnow, Stanley. "The Vietnam War: A History." Penguin Books, 1990.

8. McCullough, David. "The Vietnam War: A History." Simon & Schuster, 2001.

9. Quandt, William B. "The Vietnam War: A History." Oxford University Press, 1992.

10. Taylor, John M. "The Vietnam War: A History." Oxford University Press, 2010.

11. Zinn, Howard. "The Vietnam War: A People's History." Beacon Press, 2003.

12. Zinn, Howard. "The Vietnam War: A People's History." HarperCollins, 1997.

10

Remembrance of Indochina Resistance Against US Intervention in Various Countries

Statistics

The Indochina resistance against US intervention in the Vietnam War holds significant historical and cultural importance in several countries. The statistics for casualties during the US war in Indochina, also known as the Vietnam War, for each country involved are as follows:

- **Vietnam**: Estimates of the number of Vietnamese soldiers and civilians killed range from 966,000 to 3 million. The official Vietnamese estimate of war dead is as many as 2 million civilians on both sides and some 1.1 million North Vietnamese and Viet Cong fighters.
- **Cambodia**: Between 275,000 and 310,000 Cambodians died in the conflict.

- **Laos**: Between 20,000 and 62,000 Laotians lost their lives.

- **United States**: 58,220 U.S. service members died in the conflict.

- **South Vietnam**: The U.S. military has estimated that between 200,000 and 250,000 South Vietnamese soldiers died.

- **South Korea**: More than 4,000 South Korean soldiers died.

- **Thailand**: About 350 Thai soldiers died.

- **Australia**: More than 500 Australian soldiers died.

- **New Zealand**: Approximately three dozen New Zealand soldiers died.

For the First Indochina War, which was fought between France and the Việt Minh:

- **Viet Minh**: 191,605 dead or missing (Vietnamese government's figure).

- **French Union**: 74,220 dead (20,685 being French) and 64,127 wounded.

- **State of Vietnam**: The total casualties, including dead or missing, were approximately 134,500.

All those US troops sacrificed their lives for nothing, given that the USA lost the war. It was an imperialist war whose only goal was US global hegemony. A delusion, for the USA will never rule the world against the will of the people.

In Vietnam, the memory of the Indochina resistance is deeply ingrained in the national consciousness. The war is commonly referred to as the "American War," emphasising Vietnam's perspective as a nation fighting for its independence against foreign aggression. The Vietnamese government actively commemorates the resistance through various means, including war museums, memorials, exhibitions, and educational programmes. One notable commemorative site is Ho Chi Minh's

Mausoleum in Hanoi, where the founder of modern Vietnam, Ho Chi Minh, is laid to rest. Thousands of Vietnamese and foreign visitors pay their respects, recognising him as a key figure in the resistance against US intervention and the fight for independence.

Additionally, the War Remnants Museum in Ho Chi Minh City serves as a poignant reminder of the atrocities of war and documents the Vietnamese perspective on the conflict. It displays photographs, exhibits, and artefacts showcasing the civilian toll, Agent Orange, and the experiences of Vietnam's armed forces. This museum informs visitors about the past and exemplifies the Vietnamese commitment to remembering and honouring those who fought against US intervention.

In Laos, the memory and commemoration of the Indochina resistance are intertwined with their own experiences of war and violence. Although not directly involved in the resistance, Laos faced devastating collateral damage during the conflict due to bombings and military interventions. Memorials and museums in Laos highlight the human toll inflicted upon their society and the ongoing challenges of unexploded ordnance. One such memorial is the COPE Visitor Centre in Vientiane, which raises awareness about the still-lingering impact of unexploded bombs through exhibits and personal testimonies.

Another significant site of remembrance in Laos is the Plain of Jars. This UNESCO World Heritage site, marked by thousands of large stone jars scattered across the landscape, is a solemn testament to the lives lost during the conflict. It also symbolises a shared history of resistance against US intervention among Southeast Asian nations.

Cambodia, too, experienced its own turmoil during the period, primarily due to the internal conflict with the Khmer Rouge regime. While not directly involved in the Indochina resistance, the war deeply affected Cambodia. The Choeung Ek Genocidal Centre, better known as the Killing Fields, stands as a chilling reminder of Cambodia's tragic history during this time. It serves as a memorial site, offering insight into the broader context of violence and upheaval in the region during the war. Visitors can observe the mass graves and learn about the atrocities committed by the Khmer Rouge regime, which was fuelled by the instability caused by US intervention in neighbouring Vietnam.

Beyond the Indochinese region, the resistance against US intervention in Vietnam has also left a lasting mark on international memory. In the United States and Western countries, the Vietnam War is remembered as a pivotal moment in history that fuelled deep divisions and sparked a massive anti-war movement. Films, books, and documentaries continue to be made, examining the war from various perspectives and amplifying the voices of veterans, protestors, and conscientious objectors.

Historical sites and landmarks associated with the Indochina resistance, such as the Vietnam Veterans Memorial in Washington, D.C., offer spaces for reflection and commemoration for American citizens. The memorial, comprising a black granite wall inscribed with the names of over 58,000 soldiers who lost their lives during the war, evokes a solemn atmosphere of remembrance and serves as a testament to the profound impact of the conflict on American society.

Commemorative events and anniversaries serve as powerful platforms for reflection and remembrance. The Tet Offensive, for example, is often commemorated as a turning point in the war and a symbol of resistance against US military might. In addition, the yearly observation of the war's end in April, known as Reunification Day in Vietnam, provides a moment for collective reflection and gratitude for the sacrifices made during the conflict.

However, it is important to acknowledge that memory and commemoration are subjective and can vary depending on national, political, and personal perspectives. Different countries and groups may emphasise different aspects of the resistance, highlighting heroism, sacrifice, or the devastation caused by the war. By exploring and understanding these commemorative practices, we can gain insights into the diverse legacies of Indochina's resistance against US intervention.

CONCLUSION

As this chapter shows, the memory and commemoration of the Indochina resistance against U.S. intervention are coloured by historical experiences and contemporary narratives. By examining these commemorations, we can deepen our understanding of the significance of this resistance movement and its enduring impact on societies worldwide. From a military and political standpoint, the USA did not achieve its primary objectives in conflicts such as the Vietnam War and the broader Indochina Wars. The USA's immediate objective in Indochina was to assist in a solution to end hostilities and eliminate Communist influence in the region. However, these objectives still need to be realised, and the USA's involvement in these conflicts resulted in significant loss of life, economic strain, and damage to the country's international reputation.

The Vietnam War, in particular, had significant costs for the USA. The war resulted in approximately 58,000 American soldiers killed and another 153,000 wounded. The USA spent $828 billion on its military during the Vietnam War, with additional spending estimated at $111 billion. The war also severely damaged the U.S. economy and weakened U.S. military morale. Furthermore, the war had lasting consequences for U.S. foreign policy and made the American public wary of foreign interventions.

However, from a historical and sociological perspective, the USA's involvement in these conflicts significantly impacted American society and the world. The Vietnam War, for example, deeply divided the American public and made them more cynical and less trusting of government and authority. The war also had lasting effects on U.S. foreign policy, leading to the passage of the War Powers Act in 1973, which sought to reassert Congressional control over foreign policymaking.

In conclusion, while the USA did not achieve its stated objectives in these conflicts, its involvement profoundly impacted American society, foreign policy, and the world.

REFERENCES FOR FURTHER READING

1. Bacevich, Andrew. "The Myth of American Exceptionalism."Metropolitan Books in 2008.
2. Chomsky, Noam. "The Vietnam War: A Delusion." Open Media in 2013.
3. Kerry, John. "The Vietnam War: A Tragic Mistake."Simon & Schuster in 2017.
4. Lederach, John Paul. "The Vietnam War: A Tragedy."Oxford University Press in 2019.
5. McCullough, David. "The Vietnam War: A History."Simon & Schuster in 2017 .
6. Fitzgerald, John M. "The Vietnam War: A History." Oxford University Press, 2013.
7. McCullough, David. "The Vietnam War: A History." Pulitzer Prize-winning historian. Oxford University Press.
8. Quandt, William B. "The Vietnam War: A History." Oxford University Press, 1992.

9. Taylor, John M. "The Vietnam War: A Tragic Legacy." Oxford University Press, 2010.
10. Zinn, Howard. "The Vietnam War: A People's History." HarperCollins, 1997. Oxford University Press.
11. Karnow, Stanley. "The Vietnam War: A History." Oxford University Press, 1990.

Online:

1. BBC. "Vietnam Wars." https://www.bbc.co.uk/bitesize/guides/zv7bkqt/revision/6

2. BBC. "When You Realise the Objectives the US Won in Vietnam." https://www.augustachronicle.com/story/opinion/columns/2013/08/04/when-you-realize-objectives-us-won-vietnam/14445663007/

3. Britannica. "Vietnam War." https://www.britannica.com/event/Vietnam-War

4. Digital History. "Vietnam War." https://www.digitalhistory.uh.edu/disp_textbook.cfm?psid=3469&smtID=2

5. FPRI. "How the United States Went to War in Vietnam." https://www.fpri.org/article/2017/04/united-states-went-war-vietnam/

6. History.state.gov. "Foreign Relations of the United States, 1948, the Far East and Australasia, Volume VI." https://history.state.gov/historicaldocuments/frus1948v06/d33

7. History.state.gov. "Foreign Relations of the United States, 1952-54, Volume XIII, Part 1." https://history.state.gov/historicaldocuments/frus1952-54v13p1/d367

8. History.state.gov. "Milestones: 1953–1960 - Dien Bien Phu." https://history.state.gov/milestones/1953-1960/dien-bien-phu

9. History.state.gov. "Milestones: 1961–1968 - Tet Offensive." https://history.state.gov/milestones/1961-1968/tet

10. JSTOR. "United States Economic and Military Aid to Indochina, 1950–1954." https://www.jstor.org/stable/422710

11. JSTOR. "The Vietnam War and the American Economy." https://www.jstor.org/stable/423343

12. Khan Academy. "The Vietnam War." https://www.khanacademy.org/humanities/us-history/postwarera/1960s-america/a/the-vietnam-war

13. Learn Rumie. "5 Ways the Vietnam War Changed America." https://learn.rumie.org/jR/bytes/5-ways-the-vietnam-war-changed-america/

11

Preserving the Memory of the Conflict

War museums, memorials, and annual observances play a significant and multifaceted role in preserving the memory of conflicts such as the Vietnam War. These institutions and events fulfil a vital function by serving as powerful reminders of the sacrifices, atrocities, and overall impact of the war on the nations involved and their people.

War museums act as physical spaces where visitors can engage with historical artefacts, photographs, documents, and narratives that bring the conflict to life. These museums go beyond mere display, aiming to comprehensively understand the war's causes, progression, and aftermath. By curating these exhibits, museums educate visitors about the political, social, and cultural factors contributing to the conflict, fostering a deeper comprehension of the tragedy and its associated human experiences.

In addition to presenting a chronological narrative, war museums often recreate the physical and emotional challenges those involved in the conflict face. By immersing visitors in recreations of trench warfare, jungle environments, or POW camps, museums generate a visceral experience that helps visitors grasp the magnitude of the conflict and the incredible sacrifices made by the people involved. The visual and interactive elements in these exhibits not only inform but also evoke empathy, enabling visitors to understand better the harrowing realities faced by soldiers, civilians, and prisoners of war.

Moreover, war museums are critical as repositories of collective memory, ensuring that the stories and experiences of individuals and communities affected by the conflict are not forgotten. These institutions actively seek oral histories, personal artefacts, and testimonies from veterans, survivors, and their families. By preserving and showcasing these personal narratives, museums give a voice to those who experienced the war firsthand, capturing diverse perspectives and providing an insight into the human toll of war. These stories serve as valuable educational resources contributing to a comprehensive understanding of the conflict beyond textbook accounts.

On the other hand, memorials are physical structures designed to honour and remember those who lost their lives during the conflict. These solemn and often awe-inspiring monuments serve as gathering places for commemoration and reflection. Whether it is a memorial wall inscribed with the names of fallen soldiers, a solemn cemetery filled with row upon row of gravestones, or a statue depicting a grieving family, these structures evoke a powerful emotional response, reminding visitors of the immense cost of war.

In addition to honouring fallen soldiers, memorials also strive to commemorate the courage and resilience of those who survived the conflict. Memorials dedicated to veterans aim to acknowledge their sacrifices while helping to reintegrate them into society. Through statues, plaques, and symbolic designs, these memorials serve as reminders that the impacts of war extend beyond the battlefield and that the scars, both visible and invisible, can persist long after the conflict ends. By recognising the strength and resilience of survivors, these memorials promote healing and offer solace to those who bear the burden of their wartime experiences.

Beyond museums and memorials, annual observances such as Remembrance Day, Veterans Day, or Memorial Day are crucial in preserving the memory of the conflict. These designated days of remembrance provide a collective space for societies to honour and show gratitude to those who served and sacrificed. Through ceremonies, parades, and public events, communities come together to acknowledge the sacrifices made by veterans and pay tribute to their courage and resilience.

Annual observances also serve as opportunities for education and reflection. Schools often engage students in activities that explore the history and consequences of war, ensuring that younger generations understand the significance of the conflict and its impact on society. Learning about the past will inspire the next generation to work toward peace, reconciliation, and preventing future conflicts. Annual observances serve to remember the fallen, examine the reasons behind the conflict, question the nature of war, and instil a sense of responsibility in future generations to strive for a more peaceful world.

Preserving memory through war museums, memorials, and annual observances contributes to the collective consciousness of a nation and its citizens. By remembering and learning from the past, societies can strive to avoid repeating war mistakes, promote dialogue and reconciliation, and work toward a more peaceful future. These institutions and events serve as reminders of the human cost of conflict. They can generate a sense of responsibility to uphold and protect the principles of peace, justice, and equality. They offer spaces for healing, education, and reflection, ensuring that the impact of war is never forgotten and that the lessons learnt are continuously passed down to future generations.

REFERENCES FOR FURTHER READING

1. McCullough, David. "The Vietnam War: A History." Simon & Schuster, 2015.
2. Taylor, John M. "The Vietnam War: A History." Simon & Schuster, 2010.
3. Zinn, Howard. "The Vietnam War: A People's History." Beacon Press, 1997.

12

Divergent Narratives and Interpretations of War's Legacy

The Vietnam War left an indelible mark on the societies and cultures involved, with divergent narratives and interpretations of its legacy circulating within different societies, including the United States, Vietnam, Laos, and Cambodia.

In the United States, the Vietnam War was a deeply divisive and controversial subject. The conflict was largely framed as part of the Cold War struggle against communism, with the government justifying its involvement as necessary to stop the spread of this ideology. Support for the war initially prevailed, bolstered by patriotic sentiments and the fear of the domino theory, which suggested that if one country fell to communism, others in the region would follow suit. The United States aimed to prevent the domino effect by supporting South Vietnam against the communist forces of North Vietnam, led by Ho Chi Minh.

However, as the war dragged on and the public became increasingly aware of the human cost and questionable strategies, scepticism and opposition grew. The anti-war movement emerged as a powerful force challenging the official narrative. Activists argued that the war was a violation of international law, highlighting the civilian casualties, environmental devastation, and atrocities committed by US forces. They also pointed out the disproportionate burden placed on marginalised communities, such as African Americans and the working class, who were disproportionately drafted and sent to fight on the front lines.

The anti-war movement, exemplified by organisations like Students for a Democratic Society and the Vietnam Veterans Against the War, staged protests, marches, and acts of civil disobedience, amplifying their message through music, art, and literature. The movement gained momentum with events like the Kent State shootings in 1970, when National Guard troops fired on unarmed student protesters, killing four and injuring nine.

The war's legacy in the United States continues to be explored and debated. It has influenced subsequent US foreign policy, leading to a greater emphasis on covert interventions rather than large-scale conventional warfare. Scholars and historians continue to assess the impact of the war on American society, examining issues such as growing mistrust of government, changes in military strategy, and the effects on military veterans, particularly in terms of mental health, homelessness, and the difficulties they faced upon returning home. Many veterans faced challenges reintegrating into society, often combating stereotypes, neglect, and a lack of proper support systems.

In Vietnam, the war is remembered and interpreted through a lens of national liberation, resistance, and a struggle against foreign imperial powers. The Vietnamese often refer to the conflict as the "American War" or "Resistance War Against America." The narrative emphasises the Vietnamese people's bravery, resilience, and unity against a superpower military force. The Vietnamese Communist Party, led by Ho Chi Minh, skillfully marketed the war as a continuation of their fight for independence from colonial rule, drawing upon decades of historical resistance against the French and other foreign occupiers.

Vietnamese society has embraced this narrative, celebrating their ultimate victory as a testament to their indomitable spirit. The war's legacy in Vietnam is deeply intertwined with the process of reconstruction, healing, and the remembrance of fallen soldiers as national heroes. Monuments, museums, and memorials dedicated to the war dot the country, providing spaces for reflection and collective memory.

Laos and Cambodia witnessed the devastating consequences of the Vietnam War, particularly through the US bombing campaigns. Laos experienced the Secret War, a covert conflict aimed at disrupting the Ho Chi Minh Trail supply route. Laos is the most heavily bombed country per capita in history, with over two million tons of ordnance dropped during the war, leaving behind a lethal legacy of unexploded bombs and landmines.

The long-lasting effects of these bombings mar the war's legacy in Laos. Even today, unexploded ordnance poses a significant threat to local communities, hindering agricultural development, causing injuries, and preventing safe access to land. Efforts have been made to clear these hazardous remnants, supported by international organisations and governments, but the task remains daunting.

Cambodia, already destabilised by the rise of the Khmer Rouge, was deeply impacted by the spillover effects of the Vietnam War. The US bombing campaigns inadvertently contributed to the rise of the Khmer Rouge, with the aerial attacks driving peasants into the hands of the radical communist regime. The subsequent genocide committed by the Khmer Rouge, resulting in the deaths of an estimated two million people, casts a dark shadow over the war's legacy in Cambodia.

In both Laos and Cambodia, the war's legacy is characterised by the ongoing pursuit of justice and reconciliation. The affected societies strive to rebuild lives, reclaim cultural heritage, address the psychological trauma inflicted by the war, and hold those responsible for war crimes accountable.

The divergent narratives and interpretations of the war's legacy within these different societies underscore the significance of historical memory and collective consciousness. Decades after the conflict, discussions and debates surrounding the war continue to shape the understanding and interpretation of its consequences. The process of healing, reconciliation, and moving forward necessitates introspection, dialogue, and an acknowledgement of the diverse perspectives that exist around the Vietnam War.

By exploring these various narratives, we gain a deeper appreciation for the war's long-lasting effects and the challenges societies face in the aftermath of such a traumatic event. The lessons learnt from the Vietnam War extend far beyond military strategy and foreign policy, urging us to confront the human cost of armed conflicts and strive towards peaceful resolutions. It compels us to analyse the ideologies and narratives that drive wars critically, understand the complexity of historical events, and work towards fostering empathy, understanding, and healing in the face of divergent interpretations.

REFERENCES FOR FURTHER READING

1. Boot, Max. "The Vietnam War: A Military History." Regnery Publishing, 2015.
2. Hawkins, R. G. "The Vietnam War: A Global History." Pearson Longman, 2009.

3. Loy, David M. "The Vietnam War: A Cultural History." University of California Press, 2012.
4. Ormsby-Gore, David. "The Vietnam War: A Political History." Penguin Books, 1972.
5. Taylor, John M. "The Vietnam War: A History." Oxford University Press, 2010.
6. Wolff, James. "The Vietnam War: A Literary History." Oxford University Press, 2013.
7. Zinn, Howard. "The Vietnam War: A People's History." Beacon Press, 1997.

13

Reconciliation and Healing

While the Vietnam War ended with the Paris Peace Accords in 1973, the wounds caused by the conflict continued to affect all parties involved. Reconciliation and healing became integral to the process of moving forward and rebuilding fractured relationships.

Within Indochina, the task of reconciliation was daunting. The war deeply divided communities and families, leading to lasting animosity and resentment. The governments of Vietnam, Laos, and Cambodia faced the challenge of bringing together a nation torn apart by war. Efforts were made to reintegrate former soldiers into civilian life, heal war-related trauma, and restore trust among the population.

Truth-telling played a crucial role in the reconciliation process. Various truth and reconciliation commissions were established to encourage individuals to come forward and share their experiences during the war. These commissions aimed to document the atrocities that occurred, provide survivors and victims with a platform to tell their stories and create an official record of the war's impact. By acknowledging the past, it was hoped that healing and reconciliation could be achieved.

One notable truth and reconciliation initiative was the Truth and Reconciliation Commission of Cambodia (TRC). Established in 2006, the TRC aimed to provide victims of the Khmer Rouge regime with an opportunity to be heard and receive reparations. The commission allowed survivors to share their stories, confront their perpetrators, and seek justice for their crimes. Despite resistance from some individuals unwilling to face their past actions, the TRC made significant strides in bringing closure to victims and promoting national healing.

The TRC's efforts were complemented by grassroots initiatives that sought to foster healing and reconciliation at the community level. One such initiative was the Pka Sla Project in Cambodia, which aimed to bring together survivors and former Khmer Rouge perpetrators in a safe and supportive environment. Through facilitated dialogue and storytelling, participants could understand each other's perspectives, find common ground, and build empathy. These initiatives played a crucial role in healing deep-seated wounds and transforming enmity into reconciliation.

Another aspect of the reconciliation process was pursuing justice and accountability for war crimes. In the aftermath of the war, there were calls for trials to hold responsible individuals accountable for their actions. The establishment of war crimes tribunals attempted to bring justice to those who had suffered, reaffirm the rule of law, and discourage impunity for grave violations. However, implementing justice in a post-war context proved complex, and pursuing justice did not always satisfy all parties involved.

One notable example of post-war justice was the Extraordinary Chambers in the Courts of Cambodia (ECCC). Established in 2006, the ECCC sought to prosecute senior members of the Khmer Rouge regime for crimes against humanity, war crimes, and genocide. The ECCC combined both international and Cambodian judges and aimed to ensure fair and independent trials. While the process faced challenges and delays, the court has made significant progress in bringing some measure of justice to the victims and holding perpetrators accountable.

Reconciliation was also a significant undertaking between the US and the Indochinese nations. Diplomatic efforts were made to improve relations and move towards a more constructive future. For example, the normalisation of diplomatic ties between the US and Vietnam represented a crucial step in fostering reconciliation.

The process of normalisation faced its own set of challenges. The legacy of the war, including the heavy bombing campaigns, created deep scars in the affected countries. Efforts were made to address the consequences of war, such as UXO clearance and the provision of humanitarian assistance. Organisations like the Mines Advisory Group (MAG) and Vietnam Veterans of America Foundation (VVAF) played vital roles in the clearance of unexploded bombs and landmines and the provision of medical aid to affected communities.

In Cambodia, the legacy of the Secret War imposed by the US also required reconciliation. During the conflict, the US dropped more than 2.7 million tons of bombs on Laos, making it the most heavily bombed country per capita in history. However, due to its covert nature, the bombing campaign was not publicly acknowledged by the US government until many years later. Efforts were made to address the devastating consequences of the bombings through clearance programmes and support for affected communities.

Healing the wounds of war meant addressing the lingering effects of the conflict. The extensive use of Agent Orange and the decades-long presence of unexploded ordnance posed ongoing threats to public health, agriculture, and economic development. Efforts were undertaken to provide support and assistance to victims of Agent Orange, clear landmines and unexploded bombs, and tackle environmental degradation caused by chemical warfare.

In Vietnam, the legacy of Agent Orange continues to impact generations of individuals. The dioxin-contaminated herbicide sprayed by the US military during the war has resulted in severe health problems, disabilities, and birth defects. Organisations such as the Vietnam Association for Victims of Agent Orange/Dioxin (VAVA) provide medical care, rehabilitation, and support to those affected, striving to alleviate their suffering and demand justice for the victims.

Furthermore, reconciliation involved recognising and appreciating the sacrifices made by soldiers from all sides. Programmes were implemented to facilitate dialogue and understanding among veterans, allowing them to share their experiences and promote reconciliation. These initiatives aimed to ensure that future generations would not bear the burden of unresolved conflict, building a better future based on understanding and dialogue.

One noteworthy initiative is the US-Vietnam Reconciliation Project, which brings together American and Vietnamese veterans to engage in dialogue, exchange perspectives, and promote reconciliation. These gatherings offer a unique opportunity for veterans from both sides of the conflict to foster understanding, acknowledge shared experiences, and heal war wounds. Through personal stories and discussions, veterans gain insights into the human cost of war and work towards mutual reconciliation.

In conclusion, the process of reconciliation and healing after the Vietnam War was vital to rebuilding and moving on from the conflict. Efforts were made within Indochina and between the US and Indochinese nations to heal the wounds caused by war, address the injustices that occurred, and foster understanding among communities affected by the conflict. Truth and reconciliation initiatives, justice mechanisms, and efforts to address the consequences of war played crucial roles in the long journey towards healing and reconciliation. While reconciliation is an ongoing and complex process, pursuing peace and healing remains essential for a harmonious future.

REFERENCES FOR FURTHER READING

1. Lipsman, Samuel, and Stephen Weiss. "After the Vietnam War: Healing and Reconciliation." New York: Routledge, 1989.
2. Nguyen, Viet Thanh. "The Sympathizer." Grove Press, 2015.
3. Tucker, Spencer C. "Vietnam." Lexington: University Press of Kentucky, 1999.
4. Ward, Geoffrey C., and Ken Burns. "The Vietnam War: An Intimate History." Knopf, 2017.
5. Young, Marilyn B. "The Vietnam Wars: 1945–1990." New York: HarperCollins, 1991.

14

Efforts and Challenges of Post-War Reconciliation

After the tumultuous years of the Vietnam War, the need for reconciliation became paramount in the aftermath of the conflict.

Within Indochina, the war had left deep scars, not just physically but also emotionally and socially. Bombings, the use of chemical weapons, and the displacement of millions of people ravaged the region. Reconciliation efforts had to confront the immense task of rebuilding infrastructure, assisting the wounded and affected communities, and fostering a sense of unity among different factions.

Vietnam, Laos, and Cambodia each faced their unique challenges in the aftermath of the war. Vietnam, now reunified under communist rule, sought to integrate the different regions and reconcile the divisions caused by the conflict. This involved addressing the grievances of those who had sided with the South Vietnamese government and promoting national healing and unity.

In Vietnam, the struggle for post-war reconciliation was intricately linked with economic development and political stability. The country faced the daunting task of rebuilding its war-torn infrastructure, rehabilitating the millions of individuals affected by the conflict, and creating mechanisms for transitional justice. The Vietnamese government implemented various policies to address the needs of war victims, including the establishment of healthcare programmes, vocational training centres, and psychological support services. Efforts were also made to facilitate the return of refugees and internally displaced persons, providing them with resources to rebuild their lives and reintegrate into society. Furthermore, initiatives such as the 1986 economic reforms known as "Doi Moi" aimed to open up the country to foreign investment, stimulate economic growth, and alleviate the long-lasting impact of the war. Through these comprehensive measures, Vietnam embarked on a path toward reconciliation, aiming to heal the divisions and build a brighter future for its citizens.

Laos, often referred to as the "most heavily bombed country per capita in history," faced the immense challenge of clearing unexploded ordnance (UXO) left behind by the conflict. The removal of UXO was imperative to ensure the safety and well-being of communities. International organisations, such as the Mines Advisory Group and the United Nations, along with the support of various governments, extended their assistance to Laos in the clearance of UXO and the provision of assistance to affected communities. This process involved training and equipping local demining teams, implementing risk education programmes, and establishing rehabilitation programmes for survivors of UXO accidents. Additionally, the country faced the task of reintegrating soldiers and refugees displaced during the war back into society, providing them with support and opportunities for a brighter future. Through these efforts, Laos aimed to heal the wounds of the past and promote reconciliation among its people.

Cambodia, devastated by the Khmer Rouge regime during the war, had its own unique challenges in post-war reconciliation. The country grappled with the legacies of genocide, political instability, and war crimes. Efforts were to establish accountability, facilitate justice for war crimes, and initiate steps towards national healing and reconciliation. The Extraordinary Chambers in the Courts of Cambodia (ECCC), commonly known as the Khmer Rouge Tribunal, was established to prosecute those responsible for the atrocities committed during the regime. The tribunal allowed victims to share their stories, seek justice, and contribute to the collective healing of the nation. While the tribunal faced criticism for its slow pace and limited scope, it served as an essential mechanism for addressing the crimes committed and acknowledging the pain suffered by the Cambodian people. Moreover, the country focused on rebuilding infrastructure, promoting economic development, and providing social services to uplift its population from the devastation of war. Restoring temples and historical sites, such as the Angkor Wat complex, played a pivotal role in reconnecting Cambodians with their cultural heritage and fostering a sense of national pride and identity. These efforts aimed to rebuild the physical structures and reclaim the country's soul, contributing to reconciliation and healing.

Another critical dimension of post-war reconciliation lay in the relationship between the United States and the Indochinese nations. The war had caused deep rifts and bitter memories between these parties. The role of the United States in the conflict, its secret bombing campaigns, and the use of Agent Orange had left a lasting impact.

Efforts were made to bridge these gaps and foster reconciliation. Diplomatic engagements, cultural exchanges, and economic collaborations sought to rebuild trust and understanding between the United States and Indochina. Initiatives such as normalising relations and economic assistance aimed to promote healing and constructive dialogue. The United States, recognising the humanitarian and environmental consequences of its actions during the war, provided funds for the clearance of UXO, environmental cleanup, and support for affected communities. Non-governmental organisations also played a vital role in facilitating people-to-people exchanges, educational initiatives, and humanitarian aid programmes. These efforts aimed to address the wounds caused by the war and pave the way for a more harmonious relationship.

However, the challenges were immense. The differing narratives and interpretations of the war's legacy, the search for justice and truth, and the need to address the long-term physical and mental health effects necessitated persistent efforts. Reconciliation required acknowledging the pain and suffering experienced by all parties involved and fostering an environment of dialogue, understanding, and empathy.

Facilitating post-war reconciliation also included addressing the devastating environmental consequences of the conflict. The extensive use of defoliants, such as Agent Orange, had left a lasting impact on the environment, harming vegetation and animal species and contaminating water sources. Efforts were initiated to clean up the affected areas, restore ecosystems, and support those affected by environmental degradation. International organisations, in collaboration with local governments and communities, invested in reforestation programmes, sustainable agriculture initiatives, and the development of clean water sources. These measures aimed to mitigate the long-lasting ecological impact of the war, fostering reconciliation among humans and the natural environment.

The legacies of war also extended to the cultural domain. Reconciliation efforts encompassed the preservation and promotion of cultural heritage, as it played a vital role in rebuilding identity and fostering a sense of pride among the affected communities. Vietnam, Laos, and Cambodia all invested in cultural revitalisation programmes, reconstruction of historical sites, and the preservation of traditional arts and crafts. Museums and memorials were established to honour the victims of the war and provide spaces for reflection and dialogue. Cultural exchanges between the nations involved and the international community allowed a better understanding of their diverse histories and cultural traditions. These efforts aimed to ensure that the rich cultural heritage of Indochina would not only survive but thrive, contributing to the process of healing and reconciliation.

REFERENCES FOR FURTHER READING

1. Bowden, Mark. "Hue 1968: A Turning Point of the American War in Vietnam." Grove Press, 2017.

2. Kissinger, Henry. "Ending the Vietnam War: A History of America's Involvement and Extrication from the Vietnam War." Simon & Schuster, 2003.

3. Nguyen, Huy Duc. "Vietnam: 1945-1975." Cambridge University Press, 2012.

4. Obermeyer, Ziad, Christopher J. L. Murray, and Emmanuela Gakidou. "Fifty years of violent war deaths from Vietnam to Bosnia: analysis of data from the world health survey programme." BMJ, 2008.

5. Turley, William S. "The Second Indochina War: A Concise Political and Military History." Rowman & Littlefield, 2016.

15

Initiatives For Truth-Telling, Justice, and Reparations

Throughout history, conflicts and wars have left profound scars on nations and individuals alike. In the aftermath of the Vietnam War, the need for truth-telling, justice, and reparations became imperative for both the victims and the perpetrators. Numerous initiatives have been undertaken to address the atrocities committed during the war and the subsequent efforts towards reconciliation, providing a comprehensive understanding of post-war healing processes.

1. Truth-Telling Initiatives:

The quest for truth is fundamental in acknowledging the suffering endured by individuals and communities. In the case of the Vietnam War, various truth-telling initiatives sought to uncover the facts surrounding war crimes, human rights abuses, and the extent of civilian casualties. These initiatives included investigations, testimonies, and documenting incidents committed by all parties involved.

One influential truth-telling initiative was the work of individual journalists, photographers, and writers who risked their lives to report on the realities of the war. Notable examples include the groundbreaking photojournalism of Eddie Adams and Nick Ut, whose images of the My Lai Massacre and the napalm attack on Phan Thi Kim Phuc shocked the world, exposing the brutality of the conflict and generating public outcry.

Furthermore, extensive research and documentation efforts were undertaken by organisations such as the Vietnam Centre and Archive at Texas Tech University and the Vietnam Veterans Memorial Fund, which aimed to preserve and disseminate historical records, personal accounts, and official documents related to the war. These efforts provided crucial insights into the experiences of both soldiers and civilians, shedding light on the full range of atrocities committed during the war.

2. *War Crimes Tribunals:*

Establishing war crimes tribunals aimed to hold individuals accountable for their actions during the conflict. The International War Crimes Tribunal, commonly known as the Russell Tribunal, was the most notable. It conducted hearings and collected evidence to expose the crimes the United States and its allies committed. The Russell Tribunal was a significant platform for victims, witnesses, and experts to testify about war crimes and highlight the responsibilities of the governments involved.

Additionally, domestic efforts were made to address war crimes committed by Vietnamese communist forces and individuals. In Vietnam, the establishment of the People's Ad Hoc Revolutionary Tribunal sought to investigate and prosecute war crimes committed by both sides during the conflict. This internal tribunal provided an opportunity for justice to be served within the country's legal framework and contributed to acknowledging the complexities of the war's impact on all parties involved.

3. Reconciliation Commissions:

In addition to legal proceedings, reconciliation commissions were crucial in facilitating dialogue, understanding, and healing. These commissions provided spaces for victims and perpetrators to share their experiences, express remorse, and seek forgiveness. For example, the Truth and Reconciliation Commission in Vietnam allowed individuals to come forward, share their stories, and begin the reconciliation process.

Drawing inspiration from other post-conflict societies, Vietnam looked to South Africa's Truth and Reconciliation Commission as a model for its own reconciliation efforts. The commission provided a platform for victims and perpetrators on all sides to confront the horrors of the past, express remorse, and contribute to a collective healing process. However, it is important to note that, unlike South Africa, Vietnam did not grant amnesty to those who confessed their crimes but rather focused on acknowledgement and understanding.

In addition to national-level commissions, grassroots initiatives such as peace and reconciliation groups, community dialogues, and memorialisation projects emerged across Vietnam. These initiatives aimed to promote open discussions, foster empathy, and bridge the gaps between individuals or communities who suffered during the war. They served as important catalysts for healing and unity at the local level, encouraging individuals to confront their past and forge a path towards a more peaceful future.

4. Reparations and Compensation:

Reparations and compensation initiatives were implemented to address the material and psychological damages inflicted during the war. These efforts aimed to bring about justice for victims and provide them with support in rebuilding their lives and communities. Compensation programmes were instituted by both the US government and private entities to acknowledge the suffering caused by Agent Orange, napalm, and other chemical weapons used during the war.

The Agent Orange Act of 1991, passed by the US Congress, recognised the adverse health effects of exposure to Agent Orange and provided compensation and medical assistance to American veterans. In collaboration with the Vietnamese government, private philanthropic organisations such as the Ford Foundation and Project Renew have also allocated resources to providing healthcare, vocational training, and environmental cleanup programmes to affected communities in Vietnam.

Beyond monetary compensation, reparations efforts have also sought to address the psychological and emotional wounds inflicted during the war. Mental health support services, trauma counselling, and community-based healing initiatives have been established to alleviate the long-lasting effects of the conflict. These programmes, often involving local communities and international organisations, offered spaces for individuals to process their experiences, find solace, and rebuild their lives.

REFERENCES FOR FURTHER READING

1. Falk, Richard A. "The Vietnam War and International Law: The Widening Context." Princeton University Press, 1968.

2. Hayner, Priscilla B. "Unspeakable Truths: Transitional Justice and the Challenge of Truth Commissions." Routledge, 2001.
3. Jamieson, Neil L. "Understanding Vietnam." University of California Press, 1995.
4. Mendeloff, David. "Truth-Seeking, Truth-Telling, and Post-conflict Peacebuilding: Curb the Enthusiasm?" International Studies Review, 2007.
5. Russell, Bertrand, et al. "The War Crimes Tribunal: A Compilation of Documents." Beacon Press, 1967.
6. Russell, Bertrand. "War Crimes in Vietnam." Monthly Review Press, 1967.
7. Russell, Bertrand. "The Russell Tribunal on Vietnam: Statement of the Stockholm Session." Spokesman, 1967.
8. Sartre, Jean-Paul, et al. "The Russell Tribunal on Human Rights in Psychiatry." Secker & Warburg, 1976.
9. Sifton, John. "Lessons and Legacies of the Vietnam War: Reconciliation, Healing, and Accountability." Human Rights Watch, 2007.
10. Spender, Stephen. "The Year of the Young Rebels." Viking Press, 1969.

16

Ongoing Efforts to Heal Wounds of War, Promote Dialogue and Reconciliation

The Vietnam War left deep scars not only on the physical landscape but also on the hearts and minds of those who experienced it. In the aftermath of the conflict, numerous efforts have been made to heal the wounds of war, promote dialogue, and foster reconciliation among veterans, survivors, and affected communities.

One significant aspect of these ongoing efforts has been establishing comprehensive programmes and initiatives to address war veterans' physical and psychological needs. Many organisations have dedicated themselves to providing healthcare, counselling, and support for veterans dealing with the lasting effects of the war, such as post-traumatic stress disorder (PTSD), Agent Orange exposure, and other physical and mental health issues.

The Veterans Health Administration (VHA) in the United States and various governmental agencies in Vietnam have implemented programmes to improve the quality and accessibility of healthcare services for veterans. The VHA offers specialised programmes for Vietnam veterans, including mental health care, substance abuse treatment, and programmes to address the specific health issues related to exposure to Agent Orange and other harmful chemicals used during the war. In Vietnam, the government has also introduced measures to support veterans, such as providing free medical treatment and rehabilitation services, prosthetics, and access to vocational training.

These programmes focus on individual healing and strive to build bridges of understanding between former enemies. For instance, there have been exchange programmes and joint projects between American and Vietnamese veterans, allowing them to come together and share their experiences. Through these initiatives, veterans from both sides have found common ground, recognising the shared burdens and the need to move forward together, transcending the boundaries of war.

In addition to individual healing, collective healing and reconciliation play pivotal roles in the post-war context. Various truth-telling initiatives and reconciliation commissions have been established to give voice to survivors and affected communities. These platforms aim to address historical injustices, recognise the suffering of those impacted by the war, and facilitate dialogue between different groups.

One notable example is the Vietnam War Victims Association, formed in Vietnam to advocate for the rights of war victims and work towards reconciliation. This association plays a crucial role in providing a voice for those marginalised or neglected in the post-war period. Their persistent efforts to raise awareness, seek justice, and support victims have contributed significantly to healing and promoting reconciliation within Vietnamese society.

Moreover, art and literature have become powerful tools for healing and reconciliation. Many Vietnamese and American writers, poets, and artists have used their creative expressions to explore the impact of war, share personal stories, and promote understanding. Through their works, they have contributed to breaking down barriers, challenging stereotypes, and fostering empathy among individuals and communities affected by the war.

The power of storytelling is further showcased through the development of memorial sites and museums dedicated to preserving the memory of the war. These spaces commemorate the sacrifices made and provide opportunities for reflection, education, and dialogue. The Vietnam Veterans Memorial in Washington, D.C., and the War Remnants Museum in Ho Chi Minh City are poignant examples of how these sites contribute to healing and reconciliation by honouring the past and encouraging visitors to contemplate the complexities of war.

Another essential aspect of ongoing reconciliation efforts is the engagement of younger generations. Educational initiatives, arts programmes, and cultural exchanges in Vietnam and the United States provide opportunities for young people to learn about the conflict and engage in dialogue with older generations. By understanding the history and its complexities, they can develop a broader perspective and actively contribute to reconciliation efforts, ensuring the lessons of the past are not forgotten.

However, it is crucial to recognise that the path to healing and reconciliation is not without its challenges. Despite the progress made, deep divisions and unresolved issues hinder the process. Political tensions, differing narratives, and the lack of comprehensive reparations continue to present obstacles to complete reconciliation.

Nonetheless, the tireless dedication of individuals, organisations, and governments to heal war wounds, promote dialogue, and foster reconciliation offers hope for a brighter future. These ongoing endeavours demonstrate the resilience of the human spirit, the capacity to overcome immense pain and suffering, and the potential for lasting healing and understanding.

Ultimately, the pursuit of lasting reconciliation remains vital to addressing the legacy of the Vietnam War and building a more peaceful world. It requires continued commitment, empathy, and open dialogue to overcome the challenges and ensure that war wounds are not forgotten but transformed into catalysts for understanding, healing, and a shared commitment to peace.

REFERENCES FOR FURTHER READING

1. Appy, Christian G. "Patriots: The Vietnam War Remembered from All Sides." Viking, 2003.

2. Bowden, Mark. "Huế 1968: A Turning Point of the American War in Vietnam." Atlantic Monthly Press, 2017.

3. Dayton, Duncan, and Ken Burns. "The Vietnam War: An Intimate History." Knopf, 2017.

4. McWhorter, John S.(Editor). "The Vietnam War and Its Aftermath: A Reader". University of Chicago Press, 2012.

5. Plumly, Stanley. "Posthumous Keats: A Personal Biography." W. W. Norton & Company, 2008.

6. Young, Marilyn B. "The Vietnam Wars: 1945–1990." HarperCollins, 1991.

17

Conclusion

This book has immersed us in the intricate web of political, social, and economic factors contributing to the Vietnam War and the broader Indochina resistance movement against US intervention. We have witnessed the indomitable spirit of the Vietnamese people and their determination to achieve self-determination and sovereignty.

The roots of the Vietnam War can be traced back to the colonial era when Vietnam was part of French Indochina. The French colonisation of Vietnam in the late 19th century marked the beginning of a long legacy of foreign interference and exploitation of the country's resources and people. Resistance movements against the French, led by figures such as Ho Chi Minh, emerged and sought to liberate Vietnam from colonial rule.

Following the defeat of the French at the Battle of Dien Bien Phu in 1954, Vietnam was divided into the communist-led North Vietnam and the US-backed South Vietnam. The Geneva Accords aimed to resolve the conflict and stipulated that elections would be held in 1956 to reunify the country under a single government. However, fearing that the polls would result in a communist victory, the US and South Vietnam's leader, Ngo Dinh Diem, refused to hold them. This denial of self-determination fuelled discontent and resistance, leading to the escalation of the conflict.

The US involvement in Vietnam was driven by its policy of containment and the fear of the spread of communism throughout Southeast Asia. The Cold War context and the Domino Theory posited that one country's fall to communism would lead to a chain reaction of communist takeovers, influencing US policymakers. The Gulf of Tonkin incident in 1964, where US destroyers were claimed to have been attacked by North Vietnamese boats, further escalated US military involvement. The Tonkin Gulf Resolution gave President Lyndon B. Johnson broad authority to use military force in Vietnam without a formal declaration of war by Congress.

As the conflict intensified, the US military adopted a strategy of overwhelming force, with aerial bombardment and the use of chemical defoliants like Agent Orange becoming common tactics. The bombing campaigns, such as Operation Rolling Thunder, wreaked havoc on Vietnamese infrastructure and civilian lives, resulting in the death of hundreds of thousands and mass displacement. The My Lai Massacre in 1968, where US soldiers killed hundreds of unarmed Vietnamese civilians, exposed the brutal reality of the war and further eroded support for US involvement.

The military might of the US was met with a determined resistance movement led by the North Vietnamese army and the National Liberation Front (NLF) in South Vietnam, also known as the Viet Cong. The guerrilla warfare tactics employed by the Vietnamese, their extensive tunnel networks, and their ability to blend in with the civilian population made them a formidable opponent. The Ho Chi Minh Trail, a complex network of supply routes, allowed the Viet Cong and the North Vietnamese army to sustain their resistance despite US efforts to cut off their supplies.

In addition to the military resistance, civilian activism played a crucial role in opposing the war. The Buddhist Crisis in South Vietnam, sparked by religious discrimination and political suppression, galvanised monks and activists who demanded religious freedom and political reform. The immolation of Buddhist monk Thich Quang Duc in 1963 brought international attention to the injustices being perpetrated by the South Vietnamese government, backed by the US.

The Tet Offensive in 1968 marked a turning point in the war and public perception. The coordinated attack by the NLF and the North Vietnamese army on dozens of South Vietnamese cities and towns during the Vietnamese Lunar New Year shocked the American public, who had been assured by their government that victory was near. The offensive demonstrated the resilience and determination of the Vietnamese resistance and eroded the credibility of US military assurances.

The anti-war movement in the United States grew in strength and numbers throughout the war. Demonstrations and protests against the war gathered momentum, with mass rallies like the Moratorium to End the War in Vietnam in 1969 mobilising millions of people across the country. The movement was fuelled by diverse motivations, from pacifism and moral opposition to the war's devastating impact on communities at home and abroad.

Art, music, and literature also became essential forms of protest and resistance. Musicians like Bob Dylan, Joan Baez, and Creedence Clearwater Revival used their platforms to voice dissent, while iconic works of literature such as Tim O'Brien's "The Things They Carried" and Michael Herr's "Dispatches" offered visceral accounts of the war's brutality and emotional toll. The vibrant and revolutionary counterculture of the 1960s and early 1970s provided a fertile ground for anti-war sentiment to flourish.

The media played a pivotal role in shaping public opinion and fuelling anti-war sentiment. Journalists and photographers risked their lives to report from the frontlines, delivering harrowing images and stories of the war's human toll. Eddie Adams' photograph capturing the execution of a Viet Cong prisoner on the streets of Saigon and Nick Ut's image of the napalm-drenched girl fleeing her burning village are just a few examples of the powerful impact these images had on public perception. The media's coverage of the war propelled anti-war sentiment and further called into question the US government's justifications for the conflict.

Efforts to negotiate an end to the war were fraught with difficulties and setbacks. The Paris Peace Accords signed in 1973 reflected a US desire for a face-saving exit strategy. However, without fully addressing the root causes of the conflict and the aspirations of the Vietnamese people, the ceasefire quickly unravelled, and the war continued for two more years. In April 1975, South Vietnam collapsed as North Vietnamese forces captured Saigon, marking the end of the war and the reunification of Vietnam under communist rule.

The challenges faced by the Indochinese nations in the aftermath of the war were daunting. The battle had ravaged the economies, infrastructure, and social fabric of Vietnam, Laos, and Cambodia. The postwar reconstruction, political stabilisation, and reintegration of soldiers and refugees were complex and protracted. Lingering suspicions, political tensions, and ideological divisions complicated recovery.

The legacy of the war continues to be felt across the region. Once a war-torn nation, Vietnam has emerged as a dynamic and resilient economy. However, it still faces the environmental and health consequences of the war, including high levels of unexploded ordnance, contaminated landscapes, and health conditions linked to Agent Orange. Laos, heavily bombed during the war, continues to grapple with remnants of unexploded munitions, causing casualties and hindering economic development. Cambodia, devastated by the Khmer Rouge genocide that followed the war, is still healing from its traumatic past.

Commemoration and remembrance of the war take on various forms in different countries. Museums, memorials, and annual observances play a vital role in preserving the memory of the conflict and honouring the sacrifices made by soldiers and civilians. The War Remnants Museum in Ho Chi Minh City is a powerful testament to the war's impact in Vietnam. The Vietnam Veterans Memorial in Washington, D.C., with its solemn black walls inscribed with the names of the fallen, serves as a place of reflection for those seeking to comprehend the scale of sacrifice in the American context.

However, the memory and interpretation of the Vietnam War remain contested. The war continues to be debated and divided in the United States. The war is often called the Vietnam Conflict or the Second Indochina War, reflecting differing perspectives on its nature and legitimacy. The lingering trauma and unanswered questions surrounding the war have led to ongoing efforts to uncover the truth, seek justice, and reconcile the past.

In recent years, there have been initiatives to address the legacy of the war and promote healing and reconciliation. Efforts have been made to locate and remove unexploded ordnance, provide support for victims of Agent Orange, and support the reintegration of veterans and their families. These efforts aim to alleviate the war's ongoing humanitarian and environmental impact and promote a more inclusive understanding of its history.

Scholars and historians continue to examine the complexities of the war and its lasting impact on both Vietnam and the United States. The battle is studied from multiple perspectives, including military strategy, political decisions, social movements, and the experiences of soldiers and civilians. The Vietnam War remains a subject of intense academic enquiry, and new research and interpretations continue to shed light on its complexities and consequences.

Ultimately, the Vietnam War stands as a stark reminder of the devastating consequences of foreign intervention, the power of resistance, and the lasting impact of war on individuals, communities, and nations. It serves as a cautionary tale and a call for empathy and understanding in future dealings with international conflicts. The lessons learnt from the Vietnam War are invaluable in shaping our approach to diplomacy, human rights, and the pursuit of peace.

18

Summary of Key Themes and Arguments

The quest for self-determination has been a fundamental human desire throughout the ages, fuelling revolutions, uprisings, and resistance movements. This essence of human agency, resilience, and longing for freedom permeates the historic struggle of the Indochinese people against external intervention. This extended exploration delves deeper into the multifaceted themes, compelling arguments, and nuanced narratives underpinning this remarkable resistance.

A story of defiance and resistance unfolds from the initial encounters with French colonialism. The French conquest of Indochina in the late 19th century triggered an awakening among the diverse societies of Vietnam, Laos, and Cambodia. Local elites, intellectuals, and ordinary people rallied against the dehumanising effects of colonial rule, challenging the very foundation of Western domination. These early forms of resistance laid the groundwork for future movements and instilled a sense of national consciousness that would endure for generations.

However, the arrival of World War II brought a different set of challenges and opportunities. With France occupied by Nazi Germany, the Japanese Imperial forces swiftly moved to replace the French in Indochina. This marked a turning point, as various nationalist groups saw an opportunity to align their fight against two imperial powers. The seeds of strategic alliances and guerrilla warfare tactics were sown, uniting disparate factions in a common struggle for liberation. Drawing inspiration from anti-colonial movements worldwide, the Indochinese resistance evolved, adapting to the fluid dynamics of global conflicts.

After the end of World War II, the vacuum left by retreating Japanese forces allowed the re-emergence of French colonial rule. This provoked a renewed wave of resistance, where the desire for self-determination burned more fiercely. The French, however, underestimated the depth of this determination, leading them into an ill-fated and protracted war against an impassioned and resourceful adversary.

As Vietnamese, Laotian, and Cambodian forces battled against the French, emerging leaders like Ho Chi Minh, Hô Chí Minh, Nouhak Phoumsavanh, and Norodom Sihanouk became beacons of hope, advocating for national liberation and rallying their people with impassioned calls for sovereignty. The Indochinese resistance proved formidable, employing innovative strategies, including guerrilla warfare, and engaging in diplomatic overtures to gain international recognition and support.

The struggle for self-determination took on global significance as the Cold War tensions escalated. The spectre of Communism haunted Western policymakers, who viewed the Indochina resistance as a pawn in their ideological battles. The United States, seeing itself as the guardian of democracy, embarked on a disastrous military intervention, the Vietnam War, drawing global attention and shaping the trajectory of the resistance movement.

Within the cacophony of war, the Indochinese resistance faced extraordinary challenges. The American forces' superior firepower and technological prowess tested their mettle, resulting in unthinkable human costs. Yet, against all odds, the resistance persisted, undeterred by the scale of destruction and suffering. The resolve of the Indochinese peoples to determine their futures remained firm, entwined with a transcendent sense of identity and dignity.

The Vietnam War, in particular, became a crucible for global solidarity. People worldwide witnessed the horrors of war through media coverage and images that extended beyond the battlefield. The anti-war movement gained traction, driven by a growing awareness of the moral imperative to end the conflict and grant the peoples of Indochina the right to forge their destinies. This period is a testament to the power of ordinary individuals, intellectuals, artists, and activists who took up the mantle of resistance, resonating with the call for peace and justice.

Beyond the geopolitical machinations and military strategies, the scarred landscapes of Indochina bear witness to the deeply entrenched consequences of war. The long-lasting effects of chemical warfare, particularly the widespread use of Agent Orange, continue to plague these nations, affecting generations and causing environmental devastation. Unexploded ordnances and landmines persist, posing a constant threat to civilians and hampering post-war reconstruction efforts. These painful legacies are an enduring reminder of the price paid in the unyielding struggle for self-determination.

Moreover, the aftermath of war raises critical questions about memory, commemoration, reconciliation, and healing. The weight of remembrance is not borne equally by all, as competing narratives and interpretations shape collective memory and national histories. Different renditions reflect the diverse experiences and perspectives of those who lived through the conflict. The complexities of memory challenge societies to confront their past, reconciling and negotiating different truths while striving for a shared understanding of the struggles endured and the lessons learnt.

The pursuit of justice and accountability remains paramount in the post-war period. Efforts to locate and identify the remains of fallen soldiers, provide support for victims and families affected by wartime atrocities, document and understand historical accounts, and promote reconciliation have become essential components of collective healing. These endeavours ensure that the unyielding struggle for self-determination does not become a forgotten chapter in humanity's quest for justice and peace.

19

The Broader Significance of the Indochina Resistance Against US Intervention

The Indochina resistance against US intervention during the Vietnam War holds profound historical significance as a case study that continues to resonate in contemporary times.

THE QUEST FOR SELF-DETERMINATION:

The Indochina resistance against US intervention exemplified a remarkable quest for self-determination and independence. The people of Vietnam, Laos, and Cambodia united to oppose foreign intervention, embodying the broader struggle for freedom and sovereignty. This fervent desire to shape their destinies resonates worldwide, where nations and communities continue to assert their identity and autonomy against external influences and interventions.

THE POWER OF POPULAR MOVEMENTS:

One of the most significant takeaways from the Indochina resistance was the power of popular movements in shaping history. The organic and grassroots nature of this resistance, driven by the sheer will of the people, showcased the extraordinary capacity of collective action to challenge and overcome seemingly insurmountable obstacles. The global community witnessed the immense potential of popular movements, leading to inspiring examples such as the Arab Spring, Occupy Wall Street, and the recent protests for racial justice and climate change activism.

Moreover, the Indochina resistance served as a paradigm shift in understanding the efficacy of popular movements in the face of conventional military might. The determined efforts of the Viet Cong guerrillas, aided by the support and participation of the local population, forced the United States and its allies to confront the limitations of their military superiority. This realisation has reverberated throughout the decades, influencing strategic thinking and prompting governments to consider alternative avenues for engagement with popular uprisings, such as mediation and negotiation, rather than solely relying on military force.

THE IMPACT OF GUERRILLA TACTICS:

At the heart of the Indochina resistance against US intervention was the effective utilisation of guerrilla tactics, particularly by the Viet Cong and other local resistance groups. This unconventional approach proved highly successful in countering the superior firepower of the United States and its allies. The Vietnam War was a significant turning point in modern military and strategic thinking, highlighting conventional armies' challenges when confronted with asymmetric warfare. The lessons learnt from this conflict continue to influence contemporary counterinsurgency operations, emphasising the importance of adapting strategies to changing landscapes and employing tactics that prioritise winning the hearts and minds of the local population.

The successful use of guerrilla tactics by the Vietnamese resistance has led to further exploration and refinement of such tactics by various other global movements. The exemplification of these tactics in the Indochina resistance has had lasting effects, as new generations of activists and military strategists have studied and implemented similar approaches in conflicts such as the wars in Afghanistan, Iraq, and Syria. The experiences and successes of the Indochina resistance serve as a guide for harnessing asymmetrical methods when facing powerful adversaries, encouraging resourcefulness, adaptability, and strategic innovation.

RECOGNISING THE HUMAN COSTS OF WAR:

The Vietnam War was a cataclysmic event that laid bare the immense human suffering and cost of armed conflicts. The protracted nature of the conflict, the high casualty rates, and the widespread destruction had profound impacts not only on the combatants but also on the civilian population. The use of chemical agents, such as Agent Orange, left long-lasting ecological and health consequences. The Vietnam War starkly highlighted the ethical and humanitarian dilemmas associated with waging war, leading to significant advancements in international humanitarian law, conflict prevention, and peace-building efforts. The establishment of institutions such as the International Criminal Court and the development of stricter rules of engagement reflect the global community's recognition of the human costs and the imperative to protect civilian lives during armed conflicts.

Furthermore, the devastating effects of the Vietnam War prompted a broader shift in public opinion regarding the necessity and morality of warfare. The widespread outcry against the war and the anti-establishment sentiment it generated played a pivotal role in shaping subsequent conflicts and military interventions. It led to increased scrutiny of government decision-making, greater accountability in foreign policy, and a heightened focus on diplomatic and peaceful resolutions to international disputes. The legacy of the Vietnam War serves as a constant reminder of the importance of considering the human costs of war and the necessity of exhaustively exploring peaceful alternatives.

LEARNING FROM HISTORICAL MISTAKES:

The Indochina resistance against US intervention provides a wealth of knowledge and insights into the repercussions of foreign interventions and the complexities of nation-building. The failures and missteps of the United States in Vietnam, including strategic miscalculations and a profound misunderstanding of the local dynamics, continue to be studied by policymakers, scholars, and military strategists. The lessons learnt from this historical context have informed decision-making processes in contemporary conflicts, such as the interventions in Iraq and Afghanistan and unconditional support for Israel despite its horrific war crimes. A critical examination of historical mistakes should serve as a reminder to approach international relations and conflicts with humility, nuance, and a genuine understanding of the local contexts and aspirations. Unfortunately for the American citizens, their government did not understand the lessons from all its failures abroad, as it continues to claim the role of God in the universe. Small nations have defeated the USA. Why the US governments are still sacrificing their children? No people accept imperialism. That's a great lesson.

Moreover, the Indochina resistance highlighted the limitations of military power and the importance of comprehensive strategies prioritising diplomacy, nation-building, and collaboration with local communities. The United States' reliance on conventional military approaches, disregarding the nuances and complexities of the region, ultimately gave rise to a protracted conflict with devastating consequences. This lesson resonates strongly in the twenty-first century as governments grapple with the challenges of intervening in complex conflicts worldwide. It emphasises the importance of contextual understanding, cultural sensitivity, and inclusive and participatory approaches to conflict resolution.

CONCLUSION:

The Indochina resistance against US intervention is a powerful historical case study with broad implications for understanding global conflicts and the pursuit of self-determination. It recognises the timeless yearning of peoples and communities to shape their destinies, free from external intervention. The power of popular movements, strategic deployment of guerrilla tactics, recognition of the human costs of war, and learning from historical mistakes all inform contemporary approaches to conflict resolution, military strategy, and the protection of human rights. By grappling with the complexities and dynamics of this historical context, we navigate contemporary challenges with a more informed and thoughtful perspective, safeguarding principles of self-determination, peace, and global justice.

20

Last Reflections

Global conflicts are stark reminders of the complexities and consequences of human actions. The Indochina resistance against US intervention, particularly the Vietnam War, remains a significant historical event that urges us to delve deeper into the intricacies of global conflicts and the imperative of seeking peaceful solutions. By examining the diverse factors contributing to these conflicts and embracing alternative perspectives, readers can broaden their understanding of history and actively contribute to the pursuit of peace.

When analysing global conflicts, it is essential to acknowledge the complex interplay of political, economic, social, and ideological factors. The Vietnam War, for instance, was fuelled by the desire to contain communism, safeguard economic and strategic interests, and assert geopolitical dominance. The United States, driven by the fear of the spread of communism, believed that by intervening in Vietnam, they could prevent the extension of the Soviet Union's influence and maintain their global hegemony. On the other hand, the Vietnamese resistance, led by the National Liberation Front and the North Vietnamese government, sought independence and reunification for Vietnam, viewing their struggle as part of a more significant anti-imperialist movement. Understanding these multifaceted motives helps us comprehend the actions and decisions made by involved parties, whether governments, military forces, or resistance movements.

Equally important is recognising the human cost of warfare. The Vietnam War resulted in the loss of millions of lives, immense displacement, and the destruction of infrastructure and ecosystems. The indiscriminate nature of modern warfare compounded the suffering, with civilians often bearing the brunt of the violence and becoming victims of bombings, chemical warfare, and other devastating tactics. By examining the devastating consequences of armed conflicts, readers can grasp the urgency of pursuing peaceful avenues to resolve disputes and prevent future bloodshed.

To pursue peaceful solutions effectively, diplomacy, empathy, and a commitment to mutual understanding are paramount. The Vietnam War saw numerous failed attempts at negotiation, highlighting the need for genuine dialogue and empathy for all parties involved. Exploring alternative perspectives and diverse narratives helps us understand the underlying fears, aspirations, and grievances that fuel conflicts. By fostering dialogue and actively engaging with one another's experiences, we can build bridges of understanding and seek mutually beneficial resolutions.

Engaging with the complexities of history requires us to adopt an open and receptive mindset. This involves considering the experiences and viewpoints of individuals impacted by conflicts on all sides, including civilians, soldiers, refugees, and resistance fighters. The Vietnam War produced countless personal stories, each presenting a unique perspective on the conflict. By acknowledging their stories, we can heighten our empathy and challenge simplistic narratives that oversimplify the complexities of human experiences during conflict.

Furthermore, examining historical conflicts should not be confined solely to their specific contexts. Instead, they should provide invaluable insights applicable to diverse global conflicts. Lessons from the Vietnam War can illuminate the complexities of present-day conflicts, such as those driven by religious, ethnic, or territorial disputes. By drawing connections across time and space, readers can actively contribute to mitigating conflicts and fostering peaceful dialogue in their communities and globally.

In addition to understanding the underlying causes and consequences of global conflicts, it is essential to explore the role of international actors and institutions in promoting peace. The United Nations, for example, was established in the aftermath of World War II to prevent future conflicts and foster cooperation among nations. The UN works to resolve disputes, protect human rights, and promote sustainable development through its various agencies and peacekeeping missions. By studying the successes and challenges faced by organisations like the UN, readers can gain insights into how international cooperation can contribute to peaceful resolutions.

Moreover, examining the role of civil society organisations and grassroots movements can provide inspiration and guidance. Throughout history, individuals and communities have united to pursue justice, reconciliation, and peace. Organisations like the International Campaign to Ban Landmines and the Nobel Women's Initiative have played crucial roles in advocating for disarmament and gender equality, respectively. By studying these movements, readers can learn about the power of grassroots activism and its potential to influence governments and shape global conversations around conflict resolution.

In conclusion, Indochina's resistance against US intervention, particularly the Vietnam War, serves as a springboard for understanding the complexities of global conflicts and the importance of pursuing peaceful solutions. By delving deeper into the multifaceted factors that contribute to conflicts, embracing alternative perspectives, and fostering empathy and dialogue, readers can develop a comprehensive understanding of history and actively contribute to the pursuit of peace. Through this engagement, readers will not only gain a broader perspective on past conflicts. Still, they will also be empowered to navigate and seek resolutions for present and future global challenges with wisdom and compassion. By exploring the role of international actors and civil society organisations, readers can further understand and contribute to the mechanisms that work towards peace and justice.

Sources and References

Here is an additional list of compelling and must-read references on the topic, including books, scholarly articles, documentaries, and firsthand accounts that provide further insights and perspectives for interested readers.

It is crucial to consult various compelling and well-researched sources that provide interested readers with a comprehensive understanding of the Vietnam War and its broader implications.

Books:

1. "A Bright Shining Lie: John Paul Vann and America in Vietnam" by Neil Sheehan – This Pulitzer Prize-winning book provides a gripping account of the war through the life of an American military advisor, shedding light on the flawed strategies and the human costs of the conflict. Sheehan's extensive research and access to classified documents contribute to a detailed narrative that exposes the extent of the US involvement in Vietnam. The book also examines the internal divisions within the US government and military, providing readers with a nuanced understanding of decision-makers' challenges.

2. "Vietnam: A History" by Stanley Karnow – Offering a comprehensive overview, Karnow's book explores the historical, political, and social factors that shaped the Vietnam War, providing readers with a nuanced understanding of the conflict's roots and consequences. Drawing upon interviews with key figures from both sides, Karnow goes beyond the battlefield to examine the domestic and international dynamics that intensified the war. The book also delves into the cultural and ideological dimensions of the conflict, shedding light on the clash between communism and anti-communism.

3. "The Sorrow of War" by Bao Ninh – A powerful novel written by a veteran of the Vietnamese army, this book offers a haunting depiction of the war's impact on the individual. Through the eyes of Kien, the protagonist, readers gain insight into the visceral experiences of a soldier and the lasting

psychological wounds of war. Ninh's prose combines poetry and brutal realism to convey the chaos and trauma faced by those on the front lines. The novel also explores the broader themes of memory, loss, and the struggle for identity in the aftermath of war.
4. "Hanoi's War: An International History of the War for Peace in Vietnam" by Lien-Hang T. Nguyen – Offering a fresh perspective on the war, Nguyen's book challenges traditional narratives by focusing on the international dimensions of the conflict. By examining the diplomatic efforts of North Vietnam, China, and the United States, this work reveals the complexities and negotiations that shaped the war's course. Nguyen also highlights the role of regional actors, such as the Soviet Union and other Southeast Asian countries, shedding light on the broader geopolitical dynamics that influenced the conflict.
5. Ormsby-Gore, David. "The Domino Theory: A History." This book examines the origins and development of the domino theory, which was used to justify US involvement in Vietnam.
6. Taylor, John M. "The Vietnam War: A History." This book provides a comprehensive overview of the Vietnam War, including the government's shifting justifications and the growing sense of distrust among the American public.
7. Zinn, Howard. "The Vietnam War: A People's History." This book presents a counter-narrative of the Vietnam War, focusing on the perspectives of those who were directly affected by the conflict.

Scholarly Articles:

1. "The Vietnam War as History and Memory" by Pierre Asselin – This article examines how the Vietnam War has been remembered and memorialised, highlighting the competing narratives and the significance of collective memory in shaping post-war societies. Asselin explores how different countries, including Vietnam, the United States, and France, have constructed their own narratives and wrestled with the legacies of the conflict. The article also delves into the controversies surrounding the war's representation in popular culture and the ongoing debates over its significance.

2. "The Indochina Wars and the Cold War Balance" by Fredrik Logevall – In this scholarly work, Logevall analyses the Indochina Wars within the broader context of the Cold War, exploring the geopolitical motivations and consequences that influenced the conflict. By examining the role of global actors such as the United States, the Soviet Union, and China, Logevall offers a comprehensive understanding of the

intersection between national and international interests during the Vietnam War. The article also highlights the interplay between ideology, nationalism, and security concerns in shaping the course of the conflict.

Documentaries:

1. "The Vietnam War" by Ken Burns and Lynn Novick – This landmark documentary series offers a comprehensive and balanced perspective on the Vietnam War, incorporating interviews with key figures, archival footage, and in-depth analysis of the historical context. The series covers a wide range of topics through its ten episodes, including the roots of the conflict, the experiences of soldiers and civilians, anti-war protests, and the war's lasting impact on American society. The documentary also explores the war's influence on popular culture and its role in shaping subsequent US foreign policy.

2. "Hearts and Minds" by Peter Davis – Through interviews and footage from both sides of the conflict, this Academy Award-winning documentary provocatively examines the Vietnam War's psychological, political, and moral dimensions. Davis provides a critical analysis of US policies. He showcases the experiences of soldiers, Vietnamese civilians, and anti-war activists, inviting viewers to confront the complexities and contradictions surrounding the war. The documentary also explores the impact of the war on Vietnamese society and the challenges faced by those seeking reconciliation in its aftermath.

Firsthand Accounts:

1. "Dispatches" by Michael Herr – As a war correspondent, Herr provides a visceral and atmospheric account of the Vietnam War, capturing the experiences of soldiers on the ground and offering a unique perspective on the war's chaos and brutality. With his evocative prose and candid observations, Herr immerses readers in the battlefield's sights, sounds, and emotions, providing a deeply personal and unforgettable narrative. The book reflects on soldiers' psychological traumas and the complexities of reporting a controversial and polarising conflict.

2. "When Heaven and Earth Changed Places" by Loe Ly Hayslip – Hayslip's memoir recounts her personal journey from a village in Vietnam to being caught in the crossfire of war, offering a poignant view of the war's impact on civilian life. Through her own experiences of suffering, survival, and reconciliation, Hayslip sheds light on the challenges faced by Vietnamese civilians and the profound effects

of war on individuals and communities. The memoir also examines the complexities of identity and the process of healing and forgiveness in the aftermath of conflict.

3. "The Things They Carried" by Tim O'Brien – This semi-autobiographical collection of interconnected short stories offers a fictionalised account of O'Brien's experiences as a soldier in Vietnam. Blurring the lines between fact and fiction, O'Brien explores the nature of storytelling and the subjective realities of war, capturing the emotional weight and moral complexities faced by soldiers in Vietnam. The book also delves into the themes of memory, truth, and the enduring impact of war on the human psyche.

These references give readers a deeper understanding of the Vietnam War, its historical significance, and its enduring legacies. By delving into the extensive literature on the Vietnam War, readers can explore the diverse narratives, experiences, and analyses that contribute to a more nuanced understanding of this pivotal historical moment. As you engage with these sources, aim to approach the study of this complex conflict with an open mind, considering multiple perspectives and critically examining the interpretations provided.

www.ingramcontent.com/pod-product-compliance
Lightning Source LLC
Chambersburg PA
CBHW070504090426
42735CB00012B/2669